Mindfulness
& *the* Art *of*
Urban Living

Mindfulness
& *the* Art *of*
Urban Living

Discovering the Good Life in the City

Adam Ford

Leaping Hare Press

British Library Cataloguing-in-Publication Data
A catalogue record for this book is available from
the British Library

ISBN: 978-1-908005-77-9

This book was conceived, designed and produced by

Leaping Hare Press

Creative Director PETER BRIDGEWATER
Publisher SUSAN KELLY
Commissioning Editor MONICA PERDONI
Art Director WAYNE BLADES
Senior Editor JAYNE ANSELL
Designer GINNY ZEAL
Illustrator CLIFFORD HARPER

Printed in China
Colour Origination by Ivy Press Reprographics
Distributed worldwide (except North America) by Thames & Hudson Ltd.,
181A High Holborn, London WC1V 7QX, UK

10 9 8 7 6 5 4 3 2 1

CONTENTS

Introduction 6

CHAPTER ONE
Urban Gardens, Allotments, Bees & Chickens 24

CHAPTER TWO
A Wealth of Urban Culture 50

CHAPTER THREE
Urban Problems 72

CHAPTER FOUR
Recreation & Walking in the City 96

CHAPTER FIVE
Vistas, Cemeteries & Observatories 110

CHAPTER SIX
The Changing City: Past & Future 126

Bibliography & Further Reading 140

Acknowledgements 141

Index 142

INTRODUCTION

*The growth of great cities is currently
unstoppable; they spread outwards on the surface
of the planet like patches of lichen on a rock, visible
from space even at night, as glowing constellations
of light. Are they the future? Or are they just too big
to survive? Will they burn out, in a conflagration of
social discontent and riot, corruption, crime or plague,
ultimately unsustainable and doomed to self-destruct
from the start? We may be living on the cusp
of the biggest humanitarian disaster to befall
the world. Or perhaps we are not...*

SIDE BY SIDE

◆

The practice of mindfulness was a way of life for the Buddha and his disciples, and it continues to be followed today. It might seem strange at first to associate this peaceful practice with the noise and bustle of urban living – but that is exactly where it comes into its own.

THE BUDDHA FIRST TAUGHT MINDFULNESS two and a half thousand years ago in northern India, where new cities were growing fast, founded on an expanding iron industry. The Buddha's gospel was intended for a new generation of individuals created by city life, who wanted to let go of the trappings of organized religion (complex rituals dominated by the powerful priesthood of the caste system), to find their own way.

The practice of mindfulness is a way of living, a way of knowing oneself and the world. It involves taking stock regularly of the way things are, living consciously, becoming more aware and realistic about life. It is more than just taking time to 'stand and stare', although that is an important element. Mindfulness means taking time to meditate, setting aside moments of the day to become awake to one's physical body, emotional feelings and thoughts, discovering a renewed poise and calm. Classically, it begins with focusing on the simple activity of breathing, as life-giving air flows in and out of the lungs. To do this we need to find a comfortable private place to sit, back upright, shoulders open (but nothing forced) and let the breathing come naturally. Those of us who live in a town or city will then use this technique to go further and explore through meditation the urban environment that lies at our own doorstep. We look out imaginatively at the streets and the people with compassion and kindness, optimism and realistic hope. We are glad to be here. We resolve to take ownership of our situation and find the very best in it.

Living in an urban environment will mean something different to each of us. Dense clusters of population vary extensively in character and size from the small compact town, traditionally providing a market place for local farmers, to the vast sprawling metropolis of the modern industrialized world. Some larger towns tend these days to be referred to loosely as cities, although strictly a city is a large town that has been given the title of city by charter, especially when it contains a cathedral. In *The Art of Urban Living,* I will offer some thoughts on how to enjoy the challenges and opportunities we face when living in these exciting places.

I Love Cities

I lived in London for thirty years and have only recently moved down to Sussex, a county in the south east of England – not because I have given up on the city, but because I got married and my wife Ros is based there for work. Three of my children still live in London, and so, what with visiting them, friends and my favourite galleries, I still feel that the city is home. Living in Lewes in Sussex, just an hour from the centre of the capital, has given me an opportunity to reflect on all that I have enjoyed about living an urban life, and to bring this together with my experiences of time spent in other great cities of the world – New York and San Francisco; Paris and Prague; Sydney and Perth in Australia; Buenos Aires and Asunción in South America. All these places, and more, have strengthened my conviction that cities can bring out the very best in people, and are great places just to *be* – and to live the good life.

The Evolution of Cities

Cities have been around for a mere blink of the eye of evolutionary time. They are a recent development in human history, first appearing after the end of the last Ice Age and having a pivotal role in the emergence of civilization. The rise of agriculture, ten thousand years ago, accompanied and spurred on the growth of settled communities; with a surplus of food, new opportunities offered themselves and new trades and skills were created. It was the beginning of a process of liberation for mankind.

With the first cities we begin to see the growth of commerce and counting, and the market place becomes the focus of a new world order, a social hub for the exchange of ideas as well as for trade. Culture begins to flourish in art and music; and writing is invented. Modern man is on his way.

Like a new form of plant life, cities began very small, smaller even than a twenty-first century village; they were no more than clusters of a few dwellings drawn together for protection, perhaps against the wind and the cold, or by the discovery that cooperation when planting and harvesting crops is better than the isolation of ploughing a lonely furrow. And when the harvest was good, the community needed protection from another threat – the marauding neighbour, living by theft rather than hard work, and jealous of the stored surplus of food. Efficiency in agriculture, it seems, was the godparent of both the cooperating city community and of the protective city walls. From these small beginnings the city grew organically to become that almost unrecognizable descendent, heaving with humanity – the teeming, vehicle-polluted, skyscraper-dominated metropolis of today.

A Slow Process

The historical line of descent from small cluster of houses, through village and town, to the modern city of the twenty-first century was rarely continuous. Many places became uninhabited and fell into ruin. But they left their mark. Skara Brae, situated on the Bay o'Skaill on Mainland Orkney, off the north coast of Scotland, is a beautiful example. In 1850, a great Atlantic storm swept away thousands of tons of shoreline and uncovered this wonderfully preserved Neolithic village of eight dwellings; for forty centuries it had been lost beneath a great sand dune. Each stone-walled house has a square room with a central fire, a sleeping place to each side, stone shelves for storage and, in the corner, a simple pestle and mortar for grinding corn. Life there must have been cosy – the houses are clustered tightly together with narrow slab-covered alleyways between. Earliest signs of habitation at Skara Brae date back over five thousand years. The visitor is bound to marvel at the neatly constructed walls and wonder who it was that placed and fitted the stones with such care.

THE THREADS OF CULTURE

We have urban communities to thank for the development of culture and civilization. Museum collections and art galleries, well-proportioned town squares and ancient architecture are not add-on extras for tourists, but have always been part of the essence of city life, their roots lying far back in history.

THE GROWTH OF GREAT LIBRARIES and the patronage of the arts developed alongside the creation of beautiful buildings, elegant façades and ornamental gardens. We can only guess at what the famous Hanging Gardens of Babylon, one of the Seven Wonders of the World, must have been like; we can only speculate on the rich content of the great library of Alexandria, sadly destroyed in a dark period of prejudice. But any tourist can stroll, today, through the medieval streets

Continuous Occupation

Very few towns or cities can claim continuous occupation over a period of many millennia. One of the few, claimed by some to be the oldest continuously inhabited city on Earth, is the town of Jbeil, with a population of 40,000 people, just 40 km (25 miles) north of Beirut in Lebanon. This attractive tourist resort, with its small Mediterranean harbour and sunny beaches, is the ancient town of Byblos. Evidence of occupation covers nine thousand years, stretching back to the seventh millennium BC. The combination of a natural harbour and surrounding land of rich fertile soil has guaranteed the town's survival, and its original name highlights something important – the inextricable link we find between urban living and the development of culture. The early Greek word for papyrus (one of the town's chief exports), on which some of the earliest examples of writing can be found, was 'byblos', from which the town took its name and from which we derive, in English, the word Bible, and in French 'bibliothèque' – a library of books, some would argue, containing and representing the very essence of culture.

of Prague or Carcassonne, or marvel at the classical features of the elegant rock architecture of Petra in Jordan, the 'rose-red city half as old as time', and reflect on past times, noticing what is different, but also how some things never change.

. We are able to identify with layer upon layer of history by living in a city, to connect with generations of our forebears, enjoying the rich cultural threads that link us – art and architecture, museum, library and garden. We share with them the things they valued and we benefit enormously.

The city, often walled and protected, remained for several thousand years home for a small minority of people. The majority of mankind lived rural lives, mostly as subsistence farmers. It was the Industrial Revolution, starting in the mid-1700s, that changed all that, and it was London that grew to be the first megacity, its population rocketing from one to ten million in just a hundred years. And yet, according to The Urban Age Project (a joint collaboration between the London School of Economics and Political Science and the Deutsche Bank's Alfred Herrhausen Society), even as late as 1900 only 10 per cent of the world's population lived in cities. But the twentieth century saw a quantum explosion of urban life, so that by 2007 the number had reached 50 per cent – and the projections are startling. It is estimated that by the year 2050, as many as 75 per cent of us will live in cities. Human beings will truly have become an urban species, whether we like it or not.

Love Them or Hate Them

Public opinion has always been mixed about cities; whether they are a good or a bad thing. They evoke strong feelings, dividing people, almost tribally, into 'country folk' and 'town folk'; 'us' and 'them'. For every rural migrant who dreams of city streets 'paved with gold', there is someone else who steers well clear of the urban scene, imagining all the horror of an 'overcrowded nightmare'.

When I was a vicar in an old mill town in West Yorkshire, it always amused me to hear the opinions of local people about those who lived in London. There was distinct disdain in many voices when the topic came up. Anyone who opted to live in London 'must be mad'.

Once a year, just before Christmas, a group of wives in the parish would book a coach to take them down to the metropolis for a day's shopping. The lights of Oxford Street and the teeming stores were the perennial attraction. But then they would drop in to one or two of the more expensive shops in the West End 'for a laugh at the prices'.

They returned home late, sometimes merry and singing, convinced that anyone who actually lived in London had to be out of their mind. 'I hate all that noise – it never stops!', 'The traffic is horrendous – and the *fumes!* – enough to kill you!' And: 'If you ask directions, no one seems to speak English – they are all *foreigners* down there!' And so the stories would go on: memories rehashed amid laughter and relief to be home.

The Melting Pot

It has always been thus. One of the oldest stories in the world, of the Tower of Babel, records the fears and prejudices of tent-dwelling nomads in Mesopotamia when confronted by a brick-built city with narrow paved streets, houses several storeys high and an impressive ziggurat tower reaching to the skies. Everyone in the market place seemed to be *foreigners*, speaking different tongues. The nomads, in their fear, interpreted this to be a curse. A wrathful God must have punished the community for trying to build their way up to heaven with their great tower; and he had caused them to speak different languages so that they would not be able to understand one another. The nomads judged wrongly. They could not comprehend that a city contains a rich mixture of peoples coming together to trade, or that great architecture raises the spirits.

The different languages, and different ways, the mix of religions and colour, the '*foreigners* everywhere', are what makes a modern city vibrant – something to be celebrated, not deplored. Just think of the foods one can sample on a trip downtown: Indian, Chinese or Mexican; Turkish, Iranian or Japanese, or traditional English fish and chips, a favourite of mine!

A Matter of Opinion

The question for us, living today, is how to view the city, and we may well be ambivalent in our opinions. Is it a concrete jungle, a place of pollution and pressure, sleazy theatre of the exhausting rat race, and to be avoided at all costs? Perhaps we dream of living at the end of a lane in the country, or somewhere with trees and open fields, or on a remote island with only half a dozen neighbours.

Alternatively, could the modern city be seen as a potential urban utopia – a place rich with possibilities for enlarging the human spirit?

So, which is it? Concrete jungle or city of dreams? Hellhole or heaven?

I take, in this book, an unashamedly positive view of the city and the wealth of opportunities available to the urban dweller in the twenty-first century. I reflect mindfully on all it has to offer and look for evidence that the good life can be lived here. We need to be alert to what is happening in the world; to listen, for example, when a traveller describes Shanghai as a vibrant metropolis full of creative energy, a city looking to a future full of hope and promise. We should not be surprised when we hear someone saying how much they love living in their city, as I once was when an interviewee on

---

◆

'If you are lucky enough to have lived in Paris as a
young man, then wherever you go for the rest of your
life, it stays with you, for Paris is a moveable feast.'

ERNEST HEMINGWAY (1899–1961)
AMERICAN AUTHOR & JOURNALIST

◆

---

the radio expressed the conviction, 'I feel very alive when I am in Detroit.' On reflection, I realized that was exactly my own experience when I was teaching for a time on the Upper East Side in New York. Manhattan was invigorating, life enhancing, and I felt as though I was living in more than just a city; I was living in a great idea.

WHAT STOPS US?

Simple laziness and a lack of imagination are often our greatest enemies. We get into a rut doing the daily chores and forget to take stock of our situation. We procrastinate and tell ourselves that there will be time later to get organized. All those chains of habit become a dull weight on our days. It's easy for life's small routines to take up our time and leave us forgetting that there is a city, waiting, beyond the door.

There are deeper factors too. We may have lost belief in our own ability to find new pleasures; to stop, look up and enjoy life. Or we may have lost faith in the city as a great human enterprise, only seeing the worst in it. Practising mindfulness and becoming more aware of who and where we are can overcome these difficulties. While reflecting on our own life and the lives of those around us, we can begin to ask the question, 'How can I make good of this opportunity; how can I begin to *savour* life in the city?'

UNCOMFORTABLE FACTS

◆

Unquestionably, the modern city has problems — problems of over-crowding, of crime and terrorism, unemployment and pollution. Transport systems are strained to breaking point and the delivery of clean water or the handling of sewage, in many parts of the world, become a major challenge, exacerbating the problems of poor health.

THE PROBLEMS DO NOT END THERE: the megacity is not isolated in the way urban communities were in the past. We only have to glance at a world map with the daily flight patterns of commercial airlines laid on top of it to see a veritable spider's web of connections. A new strain of influenza could spread around the world as fast as it takes to pack your suitcase. The world itself has become a single megacity.

Before we begin our exploration of all the great opportunities that urban living has to offer, we must be realistic about the modern city; it is not at the moment a cause for celebration for a large percentage of humanity. A billion people on the planet (and the number is growing by 25 million a year) cannot enjoy the amenities of city life in the way we hope to for ourselves or for our children: they live in slums, described chillingly by Mike Davis in his book *Planet of Slums* (2006) as a means of 'warehousing this century's surplus humanity'. Any mindful approach to urban living cannot be blind to this humanitarian disaster.

The total number of slum dwellers alive on the planet today, sleeping on pavements or living in the temporary shacks of shanty towns, is already greater than was the whole population of the world in early Victorian times. The average daily income of a slum dweller is often less than those who are more affluent might spend on a newspaper. It is an appalling global problem that cannot be ignored.

'The Truth of Interbeing'

A city can never flourish in isolation – the radiating roads on a map tell this story. Examine any city in the world and it will be found to be dependent upon something beyond itself – founded on the banks of a useful river, by the sea and open to foreign business, or at the crossing of trade routes. Most important of all is the ease of access to agricultural produce: the city needs feeding.

Urban dwellers depend upon farmers – the city can never be a self-sufficient island. As the population of the world increases, this is fast becoming an urgent truth, of which the urban dweller needs to be mindful.

Thich Nhat Hanh, the famous Vietnamese Buddhist and author of *The Miracle of Mindfulness*, has coined a useful phrase – 'the truth of *interbeing*'. As human beings practising the path of mindfulness in everyday life, we discover that as individuals we cannot 'be' on our own. We are dependent on many things; on the breath flowing in and out of our bodies; on our local community, where we grow by becoming open to others, to their needs and sufferings; on 'Mother Earth', of which we are a part.

What is true of the individual is true of the city. Through mindfulness we can begin to wake up to this truth of *interbeing*. TV personality David Attenborough, campaigning tirelessly for a greater awareness of our relationship with, and responsibility for, Nature, recently reminded readers of the *Guardian* newspaper that many urban dwellers do not seem to understand the need to protect the natural world. By protecting and cherishing the natural world, we protect ourselves. It has become a truism that nothing organic has ever developed on its own: we are all part of an interconnecting and interdependent web of life. Cut down the trees and we deprive ourselves of oxygen; spray the insects and we lose our pollinated orchards of fruit trees; pollute the atmosphere and we overheat the planet.

The deeper we peer into our links with nature, the more complex the web of ecological relationships is seen to be. The rich biodiversity of the tropical forest is as essential to the sustainable life of the city dweller as it is to that of the orangutan or the glorious quetzal bird. The health of the honey bee is intimate to our own well-being.

...we cannot 'be' on our own.
We are dependent on many things...

CELEBRATING THE CITY

◆

Despite the many and daunting challenges that face urban living in the future, there is hope. People are creative, spiritual creatures and none of the problems and challenges of growing cities are in themselves insuperable.

THE ROLES OF TOWN PLANNERS, community leaders and organizers, architects and campaigners become paramount; and the future of the planet depends on how we learn, together, to live in the urban environment. And if we are worried about urban creep covering the planet in a wasteland of concrete, it is worth remembering that, despite their size, the megacities of the world still only cover 2 per cent of the Earth's surface. With a mindful and caring approach to urban development, we can get it right.

There is so much to being in a city that is exciting and wonderful, if only we can learn to set time aside and make a resolution to explore, and to make the most of what it has to offer, both of things and of people.

There are many of us who love walking and we find that there are more tracks and byways, more opportunities to stand and stare than in an equivalent area of countryside. The canals of London come to mind, where one can follow the towpath, and spend a whole day pleasurably getting acquainted with an unknown part of town: or one can stroll up Fifth

Avenue in the Big Apple, crossing into Central Park to admire from a distance the exuberant architecture of the city, its great avenues, glass and art deco.

There are parks and town squares, impressive thorough-fares or tiny alleyways with colourful shops to enjoy. We have to teach ourselves to look up and around, to stop for the odd moment and appreciate what we see. There are free concerts, and art galleries galore; places to visit to fill a lifetime. The growing taste for 'city breaks' suggests that more and more people are discovering the delight of visiting a city.

The Right Balance

Successful urban dwellers find a way to deal with the prob-lems of living in a city and we shall explore some of these in this book: how to get the balance right, for example, between anonymity (necessary for protection in the crowd) and socia-bility (essential for our well-being); how to replace suspicion and fear with a sense of togetherness and friendship. Living in the colourful melting pot of an urban community, with all its challenges, we may find that we have to overcome some prejudices. And we may feel the urge to get involved in some aspect of community action, by joining a project to 'make a difference'. Above all, the city can encourage conscious living and a truly mindful way of life – it can be exhilarating.

One thing is certain, the city is here to stay – so let us celebrate it.

CHAPTER ONE

URBAN GARDENS, ALLOTMENTS, BEES & CHICKENS

*Nothing should deter us from enjoying what
we might think of as rural pursuits when living
in the city. The tiniest space can be used for growing
flowers and shrubs or for cultivating vegetables.
Readers of Antoine de Saint-Exupéry's enchanting
tale* The Little Prince *will remember how the
Little Prince cultivated a single rose on his small home
asteroid; he loved that flower (never mind that it was a
vain rose!) — it was his and it meant the world to him.
This is how we should view the cultivatable space
available to us, and remember the Little Prince,
perhaps, when planning our own tiny urban garden.*

THE URBAN GARDEN

◆

The small courtyard behind a London terraced house is as recogniz-able in character as the white but shaded patio of a town house in Madrid, or the Parisian balcony with its wrought iron railing, tree in a pot, chair and coffee table. All of them offer wonderful opportunities for growing things.

M Y OWN EXPERIENCE has been with the London back garden. It is often no more than space for parking a bicycle or sporting a few pots of flowers and maybe a grow-bag of tomatoes; it might be big enough to host an urban sycamore tree, a friend full of character and seasonal change but littering the cracks in the paving with seedlings.

When we have decided that the space available is to be more than a yard for a dustbin and bicycle or a muddy patch for children to kick a football, planning for its future role becomes an all absorbing project. We begin to see the poten-tial of this extra living space as an extension of the house.

'I'm always talking about this!' cried a friend when stepping out into my London back garden. 'Wait while I get my camera!'

I had no idea what Anthony, a lecturer at a school of garden design, was on about; I stood, hand on spade, and wondered what aspect of my pots and paving had caught his attention.

'This happens all over London – I'm always telling my stud-ents about it,' he explained as he lined me up for a photograph.

'What does?' I asked, more than a little perplexed.

'You've dug up the children's sand pit because they don't play in it any more and you're turning it into a flower bed.' I looked down at the four sprigs of box I had planted in the corners of the raised brick area; I didn't particularly share his excitement but was interested to learn that, unknowingly, I was part of a broad urban trend.

An Outdoor Room

The clue to developing the small urban back garden is to think of it as an extra room of the house, a space to be planned and cared for just as much as the living room or kitchen. It is important to note which way it faces, when it gets the sun and when it is in shade; this will help you decide where to position a chair or bench. Personally, I like a heavy outdoor wooden seat, with flat arms broad enough to balance a mug of coffee or a glass of wine. There can be nothing more comforting than being able to relax in one's own outdoor space to catch the afternoon sun, or to sit at night beneath the coloured glow of the city sky and the odd bright star, while gazing into the warm light of one's own kitchen. What better place could there be for recollecting the day's activity in the peace of the evening, while being mindful of one's existence in the here and now?

It is extraordinary what some people manage to raise in a space not much bigger than their own sitting room – bunches of purple grapes for the autumn; crops of tomatoes producing so much fruit they have to be shared with neighbours; tubs of tulips to die for. Lovely leaves on trellises provide a gentle privacy; shy, shade-loving flowers hide in secluded corners.

One friend loves his tabletop-sized lawn; it grows in one of the most shaded gardens I know, hardly ever getting direct sun. 'How do you keep it so green?' I asked him. 'I buy a new one every spring!' he answered. 'A few rolls of turf from the local garden centre cost less than a bit of cheap carpet – much easier and more effective than trying to sow it with new seed!'

Once started, half the fun turns out to be in trying things out – shifting pots and tubs, moving the seat, building a raised bed, laying a bit of paving. No one should be too prescriptive; there is no perfect one-plan-suits-all.

Nevertheless, it is also well worth consulting the local library for ideas, or exploring the gardening section in a good bookshop. There is a flood of well-illustrated advice on the market. Some books specialize in the rooftop garden, the balcony, or even in what can be done with a window-sill.

The Tale of Virginia Creeper

A good book will also help you avoid mistakes you might regret (do you really want to cover the garden in decking, or paint all the fences Mediterranean blue?). If I had given more thought to the matter I would not, with hindsight, have planted a Virginia creeper (*Parthenocissus*) by my London kitchen window.

I loved the idea of scarlet and magenta leaves cascading down the back of the house in the autumn; but the Virginia creeper, in that particular small garden, was a mistake – I had even chosen the wrong variety. It climbed vigorously and I regularly had to cut it back from the windows, a precarious business that made the family nervous when it reached the third-floor bedrooms ('Be careful, Dad!'). The creeper went on climbing, pulling itself over the guttering and onto the roof.

The creeper spread out and started to rampage across the walls of long-suffering neighbours; they pushed armfuls away from their windows, while the creeper went on climbing and began to grope at TV aerials. By now the plant had become such a statement that I could identify the house with ease when flying in to land at Heathrow.

It had to go. Cutting it down and clearing it away was sad but necessary, and it took a week and a half out of my life! The house looked naked and in need of redecoration. Since then I have been keener to consult books before making any major changes to my garden space.

'The practice of mindfulness unveils and reveals your essential Good Heart, because it dissolves and removes the unkindness or the harm in you.'

FROM 'GLIMPSE AFTER GLIMPSE' BY SOGYAL RINPOCHE
HARPERCOLLINS, NEW YORK, 1995

MINDFUL MEDITATIONS IN THE GARDEN

❖

A garden of any size, whether urban or country, offers wonderful opportunities for mindfulness training, bringing our awareness to focus on the present moment, becoming more conscious of where we are in the here-and-now, while helping us to remember we are part of the organic web of life that wraps the planet.

THE GROWTH OF PLANTS – the simple unfurling of a leaf or the blossoming of a flower – is a mystery we too easily take for granted. It has been happening on the planet for well over a hundred million years, aeons of time before we were around to stop and take notice.

❖

'There are several reasons for keeping your eyes open when you practice meditation. With your eyes open you are less likely to fall asleep.'

FROM 'GLIMPSE AFTER GLIMPSE' BY SOGYAL RINPOCHE
HARPERCOLLINS, NEW YORK, 1995

❖

We now know the science behind the phenomenon of plant growth and can explain how the DNA, magically wrapped in the seed, the root or the bulb, carries all the information needed to create a snowdrop or a rose; we understand the process whereby leaves use photosynthesis to harvest energy from the sun and turn it into a lilac tree or a box hedge. And yet, even when all is explained, the mystery is still there. With our own garden, however small, we can stop and meditate on these things. Without photosynthesis, without the growth of plants, without a source of food, we humans wouldn't be here – our appearance on the planet was totally dependent on having something to eat.

And when the garden dies down in the autumn and the leaves fall, there is something exciting in the air that I find hard to pin down – the evenings draw in, and there is dew in the mornings; and the sweet smell of decay as plants return to the earth. I am lucky enough now to have space for a compost heap and find myself continuously astonished by the magical alchemy by which I can convert garden rubbish into next year's potatoes and flowers... Well, if I'm honest, me plus millions of creepy crawlies, several billion bacteria, and the accumulated wisdom of a billion years of evolution.

The gardener Ark Redwood, following the Zen teachings of Thich Nhat Hahn, offers many meditations in his book *The Art of Mindful Gardening* (2011). The necessity of pruning, for example, for many of us an irksome and often haphazard business, becomes with his guidance a meditation, secateurs in hand, on our relationship with vegetation: when caring for the plant 'there is no separation between the garden and the gardener', he writes. If the truth of 'interdependence' has not yet become part of our thinking, here is a great oppor-tunity to grasp it.

Bird Feeders

An added delight in a small garden or roof terrace is the opportunity to feed local birds. In fact, even without a garden I have known people who have had success from a bird feeder on a window-sill. Stories of blackbirds that come tapping on the window-pane for their raisins are not uncommon.

Cities can be surprisingly full of wild birds because the urban environment is warm, safe from most predators, and provides many sources of food. In my own West Kensington garden, the spring dawn chorus could equal anything heard in a wild wood.

A suitably placed feeder hung well above the attentions of domestic cats (particularly neighbour's cats, which somehow seem more troublesome!) will attract many regulars. In Britain, publications by the RSPB (Royal Society for the Protection of Birds) regularly contain advice on how to attract and care for wild birds – which in London means various species of tit, several types of finch, blackbirds, thrushes, starlings, robins, wrens… The list can get quite long, and may in time come to include some exotics like woodpeckers and parakeets; I was even surprised to find a South African lovebird on the feeder once – clearly an escapee. Even so, I have to admit to a frisson of envy when I remember the hummingbirds that darted and hovered around the patio of a friend who lived in the heart of San Francisco; and of the nightingales that sang in the urban garden of a former pupil of mine, in Istanbul.

A Very Special Roof Garden

As a Londoner, one of my favourite roof gardens is a totally unexpected gem that sits above the traffic near South Kensington Tube Station. It is on the top of the Ismaili Centre, opened opposite the Victoria and Albert Museum in 1985. The centre is a social, cultural and religious meeting place for the Ismaili Muslim community in the UK, and visitors are made welcome. Take a lift to the roof on the third floor and you encounter a sanctuary of calm and silence, where the sound of the traffic below is virtually inaudible. The garden is laid out formally and geometrically, drawing inspiration from the Qur'anic Gardens of Paradise (a Persian word meaning 'a park'); a fountain murmurs gently at the centre, the water flowing away in four streams. Little can be seen of London apart from the towers and dome of the V&A, which glow white after sunset. I remember fig trees and the scent of jasmine sweetening the night air. It was hard not to feel that somehow I had been transported on a magic carpet to another world.

Balance (and Imbalance) of Nature

I knew I was being successful with my bird-feeding when a sparrowhawk started to make regular calls to the nearest sycamore tree. The bird, the colour of cold iron, would make silent and swift forays across the garden, flying low like a stealth bomber. This gave me pause for thought – I was helping to feed a raptor, probably with the occasional blue tit; sad, I decided, but part of nature's chain, and in a totally different category from the unnecessary early morning killing perpetrated by the next door neighbour's cat.

The number of killings of birds by domestic cats is undisputed. Of course it is not their fault – it is in their genes and that is not an issue; but by flooding the environment with domestic cats we have caused a problem (and I come from a family who have owned several much-loved cats). In the wild, one cat family would patrol several square kilometres and their killing of birds would achieve a balance in nature (as do peregrine falcons or sparrowhawks). We who own cats need to take care of this unbalanced situation and, for instance, keep cats indoors in the early hours of spring and summer, when fledglings are learning to fly and we, still asleep, are unable to keep an eye on our felines.

ROOFTOP GARDENING

◆

Glancing up from street level, you might notice a leafy branch silhouetted against the sky, or the cheeky head of a sunflower. More and more people are discovering the delights of urban roof gardening, growing ferns, flowers and shrubs while enjoying the views over the city from their own private terrace in the sky.

WITH GROWBAGS AND POTS it is possible to cultivate a few runner beans, some tomatoes and a rich collection of herbs. One of the great advantages of roof gardens is the abundance of sunlight they experience from dawn to dusk, so that everything grows faster than down below in the garden shadows. They also attract many birds and butterflies.

A word of warning: it is, of course, worth checking with the landlord, if you have one, before cultivating the roof space. Even if it is your own roof, make sure it has load-bearing rafters and is designed to take the weight of people, pots and soil. Make sure, too, that any watering system is well under control – you don't want to come home to find dripping ceilings!

Rooftop Adventures

One of the most delightful books I have come across about urban gardening is *My Garden, The City and Me: Rooftop Adventures in the Wilds of London* (2011) by Helen Babbs. This is not a conventional 'how-to' guide to gardening but an inspiring and personal account of a young woman's own experiments with a small rooftop space (a mere 3 square metres/32 square feet) accessed from her bedroom. She begins her gardening learning curve by making a pilgrimage down to the city of Brighton and Hove on the south coast of England for 'Seedy Sunday', an annual seed-swapping event showcasing community cooperation at its best and most exuberant.

Seedy Sunday

Seedy Sunday is an event and campaign started years ago in Brighton and Hove by a local organic gardening group; it has its roots in Canada. The exchange and swapping of seeds is the main activity. It is advertised as the UK's biggest community seed swap and is also 'a campaign to protect biodiversity and protest against the increasing control of the seed supply by a handful of large companies'. Thousands of garden varieties of vegetable and fruit are in danger of disappearing (many with wonderful names such as 'Nun's Belly Button' for a bean or 'Fat Lazy Blonde' for a lettuce) unless there is action by small grass-roots growers. The campaign is spreading to other cities around the world.

I have marigolds flowering outside my own study window like glorious golden suns, grown from seeds sent to me by a friend from such a 'Seedy Sunday'.

THE ANCIENT ART OF APIARY

◆

It may come as a surprise to learn that people keep bees in town;
it is easy to imagine beehives located near open moorland with
carpets of purple heather or by flowering water meadows deep in
the countryside – but among the buildings and concrete, traffic and
pollution of a modern city?

EVEN MORE ASTONISHING is to discover beehives sitting on the roof of an urban tower block. My first awareness of bees thriving in the city was catching sight of a heavily veiled person on the roof of a terrace not far from my place of work. By strange coincidence, the person turned out to be a second cousin of mine; he had just established his first hive and was very excited about the prospect of home-grown honey.

I then became more accustomed to the idea of urban bee-keeping when an artist friend invited me to visit his collection of hives south of the River Thames. There was little room for bees where he lived with his family, so he had written tentatively to the Archbishop of Canterbury, wondering if he might place his hives in the gardens of Lambeth Palace, the archbishop's official residence: the answer was a welcoming yes!

The relationship between human beings and bees goes back a long way; one of the earliest texts referring to apiary is in Latin, in Virgil's *Georgics* Book IV. Virgil had a high and knowledgeable regard for bees, writing about 'the celestial gift of honey' and recording that 'some say that unto bees a share has been given of the Divine Intelligence…'. His advice on how to locate and develop a hive has been followed for two thousand years.

Belief in the intelligence of bees is reflected in an even older text from Sri Lanka – an early Sanskrit scripture tells of the Buddha, encouraging mindfulness and intent on awakening the whole world to the truth about reality, taking the form of a bee in order to hum the *dharma* (the Buddhist teaching) to the flowers! And a chapter in the Qur'an is dedicated to the bee, celebrating this creature as a clear demonstration of the benevolence of Allah. Then, there has always been the great respect shown for bees in the old tradition of whispering to the bees the news of a birth or a death in the family.

Letting the Bee Be

Modern research confirms the immensely important role that bees play in our lives. They are a significant link in that holistic and interconnecting web of life that wraps our planet, the biosphere. It is not just as providers of honey that they contribute to our nourishment; much of the healthy food we need depends upon them. Without the pollinating activity of bees and other pollinators, many of our crops and orchards would become useless. Anyone who decides to raise bees is committing time and energy to the health of the planet; and living in an urban environment is no bar.

The Natural Beekeeping Trust

This UK organization (there are others throughout the world) is dedicated to promoting awareness of sustainable bee-keeping, espousing the view that bees should be seen as 'sustainers of life on earth' rather than exploitable 'producers of honey'. Their site, www.naturalbeekeepingtrust.org, offers inspiring courses about rearing bees and a philosophy rich in ecology. The newcomer to apiary will quickly discover that there are some passionate on-going debates within the beekeeping world. Should swarming, for example, be encouraged? Some believe that swarming is good for bees; it breaks the cycle of the varroa mite that can cause such devastation in a hive. The Natural Beekeeping Trust supports this view, writing that 'winter survival rates are far better in colonies that have swarmed and overwintered on their own honey as opposed to sugar water or worse'. Urban beekeepers sometimes take a different view: swarming in urban surround-ings can be fraught with problems, not least being the fear aroused among the public. Urban bees need careful PR.

There are many local bee associations that welcome new members and provide help and support for those just getting started. There is nothing like a practical shared interest for bringing people together in a caring network.

A Lot to Learn

Anyone seriously interested in urban beekeeping will not make the decision lightly; there is a lot to consider. How do you protect the bees when they are hibernating and the winter weather turns cold? What is the best wood to use for constructing a hive? And what materials are best to burn to create the essential bee-calming smoke? There is a lot to learn. A good guide is *The Urban Beekeeper: A Year of Bees in the City* by Steve Benbow. It gives a month-by-month account of dos and don'ts both for the beginner and also for the established bee-keeper, by a man who has years of experience as an apiarist. Benbow moved his beekeeping from the rural county of Shropshire to the roof of a tower block in London's Bermondsey and then, by invitation, to the roof of Fortnum & Mason on Piccadilly. Today he runs thirty sites across London, including on top of the Tate Modern and Tate Britain art galleries.

London, of course, is not unique in this matter: the parks and gardens of many cities, full of flowers and trees, provide rich and varied sources of pollen and nectar. Benbow tells of visiting a beekeeper in a favela in Rio; of another who kept his hives above the fifteenth floor of a building in Manhattan; and he tells of commercial beekeepers who regularly move their hives into the centre of Berlin to harvest the nectar from flowering lime trees. The fruitful association of bees with people that can be traced back to antiquity has not ended with the growth of the modern city. Bees thrive in an urban landscape.

CHICKENS IN THE CITY

◆

I once assumed that bye-laws must exist outlawing the practice of keeping chickens in the city. I could happily dream of chickens scratching the dust contentedly in farmyards, of roosters crowing from gate posts in the rural dawn; but then I heard about people raising chickens in Brooklyn...

BROOKLYN'S CONVERTS TO CHICKEN REARING enjoy sharing their discovery with others and blog with enthusiasm about the advantages. 'Chickens – hens specifically – are the easiest and most productive pets in the world,' writes one such blogger, Jason Stroud (www.redhookchickenguy.com).

You only need 3.7 square metres (40 square feet) to rear four chickens, and each bird may lay five times a week. There is nothing like eating fresh eggs laid by your own hens – richer and tastier than eggs bought at the supermarket, and packed with Omega 3. And if you are worried about the cockerel waking furious neighbours at an unearthly hour of the morning, then the good news is that egg-laying hens are perfectly happy without a bossy and noisy male around!

With chickens, recycling rules. One of the great satisfactions of chicken husbandry lies in being able to chuck some of the kitchen waste – potato peelings, broccoli stems, the outside leaves of lettuces, uneaten fruit (not citrus) – into their run, where these leftovers are miraculously turned into fresh eggs: the joy of recycling while you watch. And if you happen to have a small vegetable patch or flower bed, chicken droppings provide one of the best fertilizers available.

Awakening with Chickens

We human beings should not think of ourselves as an isolated and superior species somehow disconnected from the rest of the planet; we are made of the same soil as that scratched by the chicken searching idly for food on a summer's day. The sense of alienation that causes us to forget our deep links with the rest of the natural world is a costly delusion. Opportunities for us to identify with nature should be valued. Crowing roosters have traditionally woken the farmer and the farmyard to the dawn; raising chickens can awaken us at an even deeper level of mindfulness.

ZEN HEN

Clea Danaan, author of *Zen and the Art of Raising Chickens* (2010) reminds us of the significant role that raising chickens can play in our efforts to improve our levels of conscious living. 'Stand in your back garden and hold a smooth, still-warm hen egg in your palm, and you find your body stills. The chatter in your mind quietens. You remember to breathe. In that moment everything "goes as it goes".'

Allotments & Communal Gardens

◆

So far we have been considering ways in which private spaces may be used for growing flowers and vegetables or raising chickens; but one of the great advantages of urban living is the chance to work with neighbours on allotments or in communal gardens.

ANYONE TRAVELLING on an overland train in a UK city has seen allotments – those neatly parcelled plots of land, divided by narrow pathways, packed with vegetables and flowers and often sporting a shed. They cluster by railway lines, by the towpaths of canals and on open wasteland.

As the train carries you away, you might just have had time to glimpse a quiet and still scene – a man stooped over his broad beans, turning the leaves, checking for blackfly; a woman gathering peas from a tidy row; regimented lines of onions and shallots; a wigwam of bamboo poles just erected for an autumn crop of runner beans with the proud gardener standing to one side, admiring his handiwork.

The attractions of allotment gardening are great – the satisfaction of growing your own fresh food and gathering it for the table; the camaraderie that often goes with sharing ground in a common and worthwhile exercise; the fresh air and sense of personal space, where you can enjoy some physical activity, quietly drink some tea (the shed often contains a kettle), and even snooze in the sun on an old discarded chair.

When I briefly owned an allotment in West Yorkshire, living in a small town with a growing family to feed, I kept things simple and cultivated only potatoes, beans, lettuce and courgettes. Oh – and tomatoes. The tomatoes were accidental and grew as weeds everywhere. I had taken local advice and enriched the plot with some bags of rich black earth from a nearby sewage farm. Apparently, tomato seeds pass right through our digestive systems unaffected!

At One with the Earth

Tilling the ground, sowing seeds in the warm earth, harvesting a crop can be wonderfully calming activities, offering a chance to think at a human unhurried pace and become more mindful of one's life and commitments: conscious living at its best. It can also be immensely therapeutic. One allotment owner told me of the real healing power that can come with reconnecting with the soil. She told me about an old couple who took over an allotment near her; they were alcoholics. The woman had a sad blotchy face, drooping and steeped in drink; her husband was totally closed up in himself, tight faced and staring at the ground. They sat on a bench with their cans of cider. Then they started to grow things – he the vegetables, and she a great bank of flowers alongside the path. They began to work with pleasure and pride. 'We all admire them; they have opened out – blossomed! And they don't drink any more.'

The early twenty-first century has witnessed a new impetus for small-scale gardening – the desire to eat organic, locally grown food, and the feeling, when faced with a world dominated by giant agri-business, that 'small is beautiful'. Added to that, allotments benefit wildlife – birds, bees, butterflies – and keep our cities breathing.

The modern urban allotment in the UK has a history that can be traced back over a thousand years to Saxon times, when communal land was shared fairly among the citizens. Nowadays the land is either privately owned or belongs to the local council, and is rented out in plots of about 250 square metres (2,700 square feet), on a yearly basis. Unfortunately, many are under threat from developers wanting to make a quick profit from the land. Local campaigners have to be alert and work hard to preserve these valuable urban spaces.

Community Gardens

A group enterprise, following a different pattern from allotments, is the community garden. Allotments are individually rented, worked and cared-for plots of land where there may be cooperation with neighbours (for bulk-buying of manure, perhaps), but there is no pressure to be sociable or to leave your own private shed (other than to keep your plot in order). The work done in a community garden – planning, planting, pest control, food gathering and so forth – is a collective enterprise enjoyed by a group of shareholders or volunteers.

The cooperative community garden pattern is favoured in Australia and in the USA. In Cleveland, Ohio, for instance, a mass of work has been done to develop vacant plots for growing vegetables. There are projects such as 'The Summer Sprouts Urban Gardening Program', 'Growing to Green' and 'Cultivating our Community'. These types of movement are also now becoming increasingly popular in the UK, as demonstrated by such successful social experiments as 'Food from the Sky', developed on the roof of a London supermarket (see box), and by the Culpeper Community Garden in Islington.

Culpeper (taking its name from the famous seventeenth-century herbalist) is manned mostly by volunteers and is an oasis in the midst of the bustle of surrounding roads and a busy shopping area. Cultivated for and by local people, it offers opportunities for gardening to disabled people and children, as well as to those who live in the neighbourhood but do not have their own gardens. Created on a patch of land that was derelict and rubbish-filled, this garden is an inspiring example of what can be done by a small band of dedicated people who care about the quality of city life.

In North America, the urban Community Garden has been bedded down for much longer than in the UK – there are an estimated 18,000 of them throughout the USA and Canada, and thousands in New York, Boston and Philadelphia alone. They are listed by the American Community Garden Association, making it easy for anyone interested to find the nearest.

A New Word on the Block

The word 'permaculture' (from permanent agriculture) was coined in the 1970s, when people were first waking up to the importance of ecology, for a new way of thinking about sustainable living and organic gardening. One definition offered of this developing philosophy, by Bill Mollison on www.permaculture.net, begins: 'Permaculture is a philosophy of working with, rather than against nature…'.

The vision has spawned many successful community experiments around the world, such as 'Food from the Sky' in Crouch End, North London. An area of 450 square metres (4,850 square feet) of garden has been developed by a cooperative community venture on the roof of a local supermarket; they sell their produce – vegetables, fruits, flowers, herbs and even mushrooms – in the store 10 metres (33 feet) below (transport food-miles, eat your hearts out!) They harvest rainwater and compost the supermarket waste. The roof also acts as an educational project, teaching new skills to young and old.

Each garden has its own ethos; some are dedicated to providing open green space for local urban dwellers, others concentrate on flowers, or ecological and organic vegetable growing. The Clinton Street Garden in the middle of Manhattan, New York, is an architect-driven project, which, while growing vegetables, has an overriding and strong vision for education and a desire to increase public awareness of ecological issues.

GUERRILLA GARDENING & SEED BOMBS

If a patch of tulips has ever caught your attention, growing unexpectedly at the foot of a tree by the gutter of a busy urban thoroughfare, or a small cloud of love-in-a-mist, or wallflowers, or pansies, it is very likely that a guerrilla gardener has been at work.

GUERRILLA GARDENING BEGAN, it is claimed, in 1973 in New York with the Green Guerillas who took over a patch of derelict private land and made it bloom (see www.greenguerillas.org). Volunteers still care for the space and it has now come under the protection of the Parks Department. The remote adopted godparents of the movement are the seventeenth-century English activist Gerrard Winstanley and Johnny 'Appleseed' Chapman of Ohio in the nineteenth century. The former, a leader of the 'True Levellers', a group of protesters with a philosophy often described as a sort of Christian Communism, illicitly took over public land for cultivation with crops; whereas the latter, a nurseryman, became the centre of a romantic American legend, scattering apple seeds at random wherever he travelled in the Eastern States of Ohio and Pennsylvania.

One of the simpler techniques of guerrilla gardening is reminiscent of Johnny Appleseed – the use of an innocent weapon called the seed bomb, a home-made ball of clay mixed with organic compost, bio-friendly fertilizer and the seeds of flowers gathered manually. The bomb is lobbed onto the neglected land and nature then takes over.

Good Intentions

Guerrilla gardening is an umbrella term, covering a range of activities by those individuals who make seed bombs or plant flowers in small public patches of earth to those of highly motivated groups who illicitly adopt abandoned or neglected land, derelict building sites or fringe wasteland and cultivate it for the benefit of all. The philosophy is eco-friendly and vegetables are grown organically. Technically, the work of guerrilla gardeners is illegal, but the aims of the movement are so self-evidentially peaceful – wishing to beautify areas that otherwise have been forgotten – that many urban councils are happy to endorse their activity.

The philosophy [of guerilla gardening] is eco-friendly and vegetables are grown organically.

CHAPTER TWO

A WEALTH OF URBAN CULTURE

*Cities have always been centres of culture,
attracting visionary builders, stonemasons and other
craftsmen; great artists and their patrons; landscape
gardeners and park designers. An awareness of beauty
and a mindful concern for the urban environment have
been midwives to all the rich cultural creativity.
Valuable collections of books and historical artefacts
gravitate towards cities whose libraries and museums
then become famous. Ever since the Hanging Gardens
of Babylon, the Colosseum in Rome or the Great
Library of Alexandria drew visitors from afar, urban
centres have flourished – they have so much to offer
both the tourist and the mindful city dweller.*

ART GALLERIES & MUSEUMS

Visiting an art gallery or museum is an art in itself. It involves far more than merely strolling around blankly gazing at all there is to view. One sees many tired visitors passively exhausting themselves as they drift from room to room, looking and looking but not really seeing anything.

P UBLIC ART GALLERIES are among the most valuable facilities that a city has to offer; and yet how many people, I wonder, have been put off art exhibitions for life by being dragged, when children, around gallery after gallery, by well-intentioned parents with an educational agenda? And how many lost interest during their school days after being left with questionnaires on clipboards by teachers who then sloped off for coffee?

We have to be careful when extolling the values of art galleries; tastes and experiences differ, and boredom thresholds vary. It takes time to learn how to use a gallery and for many, it is an acquired taste. A work of art that moves one person deeply can be a 'dry as dust' experience for another.

Emma Darwin, wife of Charles Darwin of evolutionary fame, was brutally honest in her private journals about the art she was expected to see and appreciate on the Grand Tour; 'Another day of picture staring!' she noted in exhaustion and annoyance. She and her sister dutifully did the rounds of the galleries of Turin, but Emma 'did not care for any of them much'. She refused to gush over famous pictures, however much they were praised in guidebooks, and dismissed some galleries as 'hum' – the family word for humbug (an observation recorded in Edna Healey's 2001 biography *Emma Darwin*).

Great Expectations

One of the obstacles to a good gallery visit is that we may expect too much, both of the gallery and of ourselves. Given that we probably do not visit art galleries as often as we would like, we are inclined to try to see everything. The outcome is tired feet, possibly a stiff back, and an addled, over-saturated brain. We have 'done' the gallery – and done ourselves in, into the bargain.

One of my favourite places to visit in London is the Royal Academy in Burlington House, Piccadilly, where they have a rich programme of exhibitions. My own tried and tested method is to approach an exhibition at speed. I do a fast twenty-minute tour to see what is there, not dawdling or stopping, just letting my eyes slide over everything. Then I go and linger over a cup of coffee, letting my mind wander back around the gallery to see what pops up, what struck me.

Rested and invigorated, I return to the gallery to revisit no more than half a dozen exhibits, to stand or sit in front of them and mindfully explore the composition, the colour. Sometimes I might just focus on one.

Reviewing the Gallery Experience

If I have time – and it is worth finding the time – I make a point of walking at least part of the way home. Until recently I lived in Hammersmith, and the walk took me down Piccadilly into Hyde Park, which has some great trees, water features and wide-open spaces. From there I would walk on through Kensington Gardens, where you have the feeling of rising above London, looking out over its buildings and

---

Taking Time Out with Hockney

I recently visited a massive exhibition of David Hockney's painting at the Royal Academy in London, and returned twice in the following weeks. He experiments with different mediums, including a whole gallery of pictures produced on his iPad. But what struck me most was his interpretation of landscape. I revisited one picture several times (A Closer Winter Tunnel, February–March 2006) to absorb its astonishing colours. A tree-lined lane stretches away between fields to left and right; it is painted on six canvases, has leafless tree trunks in lilac and mauve, and a ploughed field in bold pink. The colours seemed wrong at first and then, as they grew on me, they became right. There is far more colour in nature than we normally register. Time spent meditating on this picture has helped me look at a landscape with new eyes, more mindfully.

towers, glimpses of the Albert Hall and Albert Memorial appearing beyond the avenues of plane trees. This walk gives the gallery experience time to sink in, and me a chance to recall and memorize whatever works I had found intriguing or moving. Taken this way, the experience can be both exhilarating and memorable.

'Don't try to do too much' should be the watchword. Give yourself time to be mindful of the experience. I became even more convinced of the value of this method when staying with friends in Washington, DC. I spent a day walking around the city, viewing the Lincoln Memorial, exploring the Smithsonian Space Museum – being a real tourist. I also wanted to visit the National Art Gallery but got my timing wrong and arrived just 15 minutes before it closed. What to do? I opted to move into sharp focus, strode fast into the gallery, selected a picture that caught my eye and let it sink in for a few minutes. It was a van Gogh, a flowery painting of roses, all white with hints of peppermint green. I loved it – and I can recall it clearly to this day.

◆

'The life of our city is rich in poetic and marvellous subjects. We are enveloped and steeped as though in an atmosphere of the marvellous: but we do not notice it.'

CHARLES BAUDELAIRE (1821–67)
FRENCH POET & ESSAYIST

◆

Mindfulness at the Museum

The same rule applies, I find, to visiting a museum; enjoy one section or even just one exhibit, savouring it in memory; the cabinet of Islamic bowls, the Persian miniatures or the fossilized dinosaur eggs from China. Trying to take in all the exhibits exhausts the mind (well – my mind anyway!). Museums have changed over the last half-century. Three words that might have been associated with many of them in the past would be 'dry', 'dust' and 'dead'; but a new generation of inspired curators has changed that. Science museums have 'hands on' exhibits that enthral children; displays are clearly labelled with the sort of information one wants; and (very important) they are well lit. They have become in many cases centres of excellence for education, places well worth visiting. Many now advertise late opening hours to help accommodate those whose time is tied up during the day. They have become visitor friendly.

It can give a particular spur to the imagination to visit a museum collection that you normally might ignore. Years ago, while in New York, I was taken by a former pupil of mine to examine an extraordinary and thought-provoking collection of letters written by Franz Kafka (one of my favourite authors) at the Jewish Museum. There was an interesting debate between us as to whether or not they should have been on show, because Kafka had left instructions in his will that they should be destroyed.

MAKING A DAY OF IT

◆

A good gallery visit can involve much more than just art. It will add greatly to the experience if we can make something of a pilgrimage of it, walking to the gallery perhaps through a park, and giving ourselves time to pause and reflect over lunch or a cup of coffee.

THE ART GALLERY OF NEW SOUTH WALES in Sydney, for example, quite apart from its wonderful collection of Australian art, is also a great place to eat. I can think of no more pleasant way to enjoy a day in Sydney than one spent, at first, strolling through the richly planted Botanic Gardens, with views of the harbour, the famous bridge and the opera house, and the high-rise buildings of the commercial district; stopping for a break in the café there, while getting to know some of the collection of Australian plants and trees. First-time visitors will marvel, too, at the enormous colony of fruit bats the size of rabbits, hanging from some of the branches, wrapped in their leathery wings like extras for a vampire film.

From the Botanic Gardens, it is a short walk to the Art Gallery of NSW. It is cool inside and a fast tour will quickly give you a taste of the riches to be contemplated in the afternoon. Then lunch, eaten in the gallery's excellent restaurant, is one of the high points of the day. A date with a friend makes the occasion even more of a celebration. What is true in Sydney is equally true elsewhere. Of all the cities around the world I have visited, from Paris to Perth, I cannot think of one where it is not possible to enjoy lunch and a good walk as part of the whole experience of visiting an art gallery.

Botanical Gardens

I find that when visiting a new city, it is well worth enquiring whether it has its own botanical gardens. I have already mentioned the beautiful gardens in the heart of Sydney, which repay visiting again and again. But every botanical garden has its own character and is a reminder that the city is a relatively recent interruption in the rich biodiversity of the planet. 'We were here long before you' is the silent message of many of the plants and trees. This is particularly true of the Kirstenbosch Gardens in Cape Town, situated on the eastern slopes of Table Mountain. They have a wonderful collection of cycads, ancient pre-flowering plants of the southern hemisphere, and of colourful proteas, whose ancestors grew in Gondwanaland 300 million years ago and which still look strange to my northern eyes.

In Singapore, it is the almost unnatural colours and shapes of orchids that grab the attention in the hot humid air; while in Asunción, Paraguay, the Jardin Botánico sports a collection of enormous tropical trees and some wild undergrowth, with a great many South American birds including pampas woodpeckers, red-crested cardinals, canary-winged parakeets and tiny masked gnatcatchers.

The Botanical Gardens at Kew

My favourite, however, are the Royal Botanical Gardens at Kew in London, containing one of the oldest plant collections in the world, and now with its associated gardens at Wakehurst Place, the leader in the field for protecting the biodiversity of the planet. Their seed bank is prodigious and doing something important for the planet, by storing seeds of over a million plants from all over the world to ensure their survival in the face of increasing threat of habitat loss due to human activity.

I have roamed round these glorious gardens innumerable times. It was here that I learned to stand and admire individual trees and to discover, for example, that there is more to the oak than meets the eye. I had always thought that an oak was an oak – and that was that. Then I learned that there are two oak species in England – the English oak, whose acorns are on stalks, and the sessile oak, whose acorns have no stalks (sessile meaning stalkless). It was while wandering around Kew Gardens that I discovered the Quercus (oak) species did not stop there, but that there are dozens of different types of oak, hundreds, in fact – Hungarian oaks, Turkish oaks, oaks that go red in the autumn, oaks that look like poplar trees… The list goes on. Many of them grow at Kew and it is easy to identify them (as in most botanical gardens) by their discreet name tabs. It is wonderful to have discovered that there is such a rich diversity in the wilds of nature by simply becoming more aware of some trees in the heart of the city.

I notice as I stroll round these Botanical Gardens that there is an excellent play centre for children and now young mothers investing in an annual subscription meet friends for coffee while the toddlers play in safety. To be able to let children run free on the open grass among the trees adds a new, welcome and refreshing dimension to city life.

This gathering of young families in parks and zoos and public gardens is not just good for urban children – it is also liberating for their mothers and fathers, who might otherwise feel cooped up at home without company, many without a garden or access to an outdoor play space. To be able to picnic and gossip with friends while the children play safely together in the open air, is an invaluable freedom, to be cherished by any urban community.

OUT TO LUNCH

My visits to Kew often finish up in the marvellous café in the orangery: a bowl of soup, some crusty bread, a bottle of ale, then coffee – what could be better? Across the grass from the orangery, a Wollemi pine ('dinosaur tree') is now well established; discovered less than twenty years ago in a remote valley of the Blue Mountains in New South Wales, this primeval 'fossil' tree, temporarily fenced in for protection, is flourishing and getting bigger every time I see it.

MAKING TIME TO LINGER

◆

Living in a city can be expensive and it becomes important for most of us that we find things to do that do not cost too much money. Many art galleries and museum collections welcome visitors without charge and many music venues are free.

A LOCAL CITY ENTERTAINMENT GUIDE will identify venues for you – there may be more than you think. One of the finest spots in London is at Covent Garden (the name harking back to the days before Henry VIII's dissolution of the monasteries, when the land was a garden owned by Westminster Abbey and its associated convent). Up until 1974, Covent Garden was famous for its fruit and vegetable market, but that has now been relocated and the piazza is dedicated to the entertainment of visitors and tourists, with shops, refreshments and street performers.

In the evolution of cities, the creation of the piazza – the open town square – has to be one of the most significant of developments, bringing space and elegance into the bustle of urban life. It was the architect Inigo Jones who, in 1630, introduced the piazza to London. A follower of Palladio's simple classical style, he was particularly struck by the Italian idea of an open urban square. His first piazza was Covent Garden. We benefit from it today – it is a place to stop and rest, watch the crowds and listen to the music of buskers.

The Piazza

The public space in an Italian town is known as a piazza and its architectural roots can be traced back two thousand years to Roman times. Although often translated into English as a 'town square', it is rarely that shape. Enthusiasm for the piazza was revived in the Renaissance; a place for meeting people, for markets and for political or religious gatherings. 'I'll meet you in the piazza' is an oft-quoted line – probably millions of times a year in Italy.

People Watching

While sitting in a town square, the gentle art of people watching – marvelling at the seemingly infinite number of different faces – can become a mindful meditation in itself. For this, you need to make time to linger. Following the movement of the crowd from your vantage point, as it flows in and out of the square, is rather like focusing on your breath, that classic mindfulness technique. You pay attention to the movement of pedestrians, 'inhaled' from the surrounding streets, held by the attractions of the square, then 'exhaled' as they wander on. You begin to get a feel of the living city, breathing to its own rhythm in the present moment, of its colour and rich diversity while becoming more aware of its true reality and vitality. You are glad to be here.

Your attention shifts from the crowds to the street performers, violinists perhaps, clarinet players or singers. A coin thrown into the music case is all it costs, and your spirits are lifted by attending to and enjoying some genuine talent. There will be magicians too; conjurors, mime artists, jugglers and comedians. I am always baffled by those artists who, sprayed white or bronze, manage to hold a still pose for hours, appearing to be a piece of solid marble or a bronze sculpture and resisting the joking distractions of onlookers

I was wonderfully entertained once at The Edinburgh Festival (which includes much street theatre) by a clown on tall stilts – he 'hid' in waiting behind a drainpipe, then as an unsuspecting pedestrian passed by, he would emerge from the shadows and follow them, doing an exaggerated imitation of their walk. The audience in the nearby street café loved it and the 'victim' was often unaware of what was happening, until something made them suspect and turn – and laugh.

The 'Happening'

Good street theatre can have remarkable and unintended consequences. In 1970, when I was vicar of a town in Yorkshire, a memorable event took place; it was called a 'Happening'. The town was somewhat dispirited at the time, unemployment was rising, and buildings were still shrouded in the black grime of the industrial revolution. Not a place to visit for a 'day out'; but that summer a band of students from Leeds

University applied for a grant from the Arts Council to stage a 'Happening', and the stage they chose was my own town. For a week, the town exploded with concerts, street theatre, buskers and all sorts of unexpected delights.

That 'Happening' was the beginning of a rejuvenation of that town – people who had flocked to the event later moved into the area, buying and doing up the cheap properties, realizing the wonderful potential of the town. Government grants for cleaning the buildings were applied for and won, the local stone revealing its golden honey colour so long hidden by factory soot. The town never looked back.

Street theatre can transform the mood of a large city, just as much as it can in a smaller town. The great festivals and carnivals in cities like Rio or Edinburgh, New Orleans or London's Notting Hill all bear witness to that.

Fringe Theatre

Anyone living on a tight budget will probably find making a regular trip to the theatre dauntingly expensive. In that case, it is worth checking out the fringe theatre venues in your neighbourhood. The experience in London is more intimate than a seat in the circle or even in the stalls in the West End. The actors will be close enough to touch; you pull in your knees and feel part of the action. The visit will be memorable.

Cool Cathedrals

Free music is not only to be found in piazzas; many city churches and cathedrals have lunch-time concerts for which you make a donation. Or there is the religious office of sung evensong – one of the most peaceful and uplifting experiences you can enjoy in a city.

The singing of a well-trained choir opens up the deep spaces of a cathedral or abbey for contemplation, the sound soaring high between the pillars to the clerestory windows far above. When you know the music and you know what's coming next, the anticipation is quite electrifying (Allegri's Miserere comes to mind in this context). The pattern of evensong laid out in the Book of Common Prayer, its choreography, is a wonderfully shaped mixture of word, prayer and anthem. It is called the liturgy, originally from Greek and meaning 'the work of the people' – so we are encouraged to let our own contemplations go with the flow of the singing, contributing our own meditative 'work' to the offering. The interplay of voices between the cleric conducting the service and the choir, in prayers composed as sung versicles and responses, has the rhythm of a mindful conversation, thoughtful and measured.

There is something about religious buildings the world over – spaces dedicated to prayer and contemplation, whether mosque, synagogue or cathedral – that generates a mood of mindfulness. It is not important whether you are a believer in that particular faith tradition or not, the place has its own quiet genius – somewhere to seek coolness in the heat of the day after the toil of shopping, or to sit and gaze at the medieval coloured glass or upward to the high roof beams.

Powerful Messages

It is always worth spending time in a large cathedral, exploring the transepts, side chapels and aisles. There may be an imaginative exhibit on show. Walking around the cathedral of Saint John the Divine in Manhattan years ago, I discovered a massive rock crystal mounted on a pedestal; a piece of American geology, unexpected and arresting. The inscription explained that it was 200 million years old. What a marvellous way to introduce the idea to the worshipping congregation that the world we inhabit is *ancient* and that creation happened in the deep time of the remote past and not just 6,000 years ago, as some fundamentalist Christians assert!

A helpful guide at that cathedral instructed me to jump straight on a bus and visit The Metropolitan Museum of Art to see a collection of photographs by the great American photographer Richard Avedon, another exhibit that struck me forcibly. They were all of weather-worn faces, portraits of the marginalized, of tramps and winos, drifters and the destitute. Remarkably and beautifully, the photographer had captured something of the essential nobility and inner dignity of people despite the poverty of their lives, the suffering they had endured. It seemed to me that this exhibition proclaimed a

Christian message about the link between nobility and vulner-
ability in human beings more powerfully than a hundred
sermons in a cathedral.

History Hunting

Every city cathedral has its own unique character and is a
space worth exploring. The great medieval cathedral in Seville
(said to be the largest Gothic cathedral in the world), built in
the fifteenth century, has an ornate bell tower that was originally the minaret of an earlier, twelfth-century mosque. The
forecourt of the original mosque is also preserved, a rectan-
gular pattern of orange trees set in a grid of irrigation
channels. It is a cool and shaded place, where Muslim wor-
shippers would wash before prayer, and in which today we
might contemplate the history of this wonderful building, and
the interplay of cultures, Muslim and Christian, that have
contributed to making the city what it is today.

Cathedrals and mosques, it seems, are great places to dig
into the history of a city. In Istanbul, we find a similar transforming process has taken place in a landmark building, but in
the reverse direction of that found in Seville's Cathedral –
in 1453, Istanbul (then called Constantinople) fell to the
Ottomans and its great Byzantine church, the Hagia Sophia,
was converted into a mosque; the domes and minarets of this
building have become an iconic image of the renamed Istanbul
and of Turkish culture. It is now a museum.

EATING OUT – OR IN

Going out for a meal can be more than just finding something to grab when hungry; it can become a small celebration in itself – taking time to think, consult the menu, order and eat, especially when it brings family together, or friends. It is a cultured activity and it does not need to be expensive.

IT IS SURELY TRUE THAT THE URBAN DWELLER has a better choice of places to eat out than their country cousin. When I was younger, no one I knew ate out on a regular basis – money was in short supply and it was considerably cheaper to eat at home. Nowadays, things have changed – London has become more like Paris, and my children's generation seem to eat out all the time, some of them even having flats without kitchens. I have picked up the habit and become quite a connoisseur of the pub meals I consume!

Pub lunches or pub suppers are often very reasonably priced; and the choice of economic restaurants in a city like London is vast. Whether you want an Indian hot rogan josh, a tasty Greek lamb stew, Italian spaghetti or something more exotic, it is probably there for the asking, with delicious vegetarian alternatives – and all of them just round the corner.

Despite their recent blossoming popularity, places to eat out in the city are not a recent invention; Charles Dickens refers to the 'Slap-Bang', a downtown eating house, in his

novel *Bleak House*, and he often refers to coffee houses. We might think that sending out for a meal is something new; a Chinese takeaway or pizza arriving by moped twenty minutes after being ordered. But in the same book, Dickens writes about the dry old lawyer Mr Tulkinghorn, enjoying his wine by the open window on a hot summer's night, 'when he dines alone in chambers, as he has dined today, and has his bit of fish and his steak or chicken brought in from the coffee house…'.

Farmers' Markets

If you decide to have a large family gathering at home, the urban dweller has the advantage of a choice of Farmers' Markets from which to purchase the food. They are a fairly recent development in the UK (a revival of the great markets to be found in medieval cities throughout Europe), responding to the desire of urban citizens to buy organic food grown locally with a minimum of food miles. Food shopping becomes a real pleasure at a Farmers' Market, where the very nature of the temporary stalls seem designed to generate friendliness – vegetable stalls piled with produce as fresh as it would be if you lived in the country or had grown it in your own garden; mouth-watering bread in all shapes and sizes, baked from rye,

Despite their recent blossoming popularity, places to eat out in the city are not a recent invention.

barley or wheat, some with sesame or sunflower seeds; trestle tables covered in all manner of tempting cheeses. Stacks of fruit proclaim health and freshness. Farmers' Markets provide such an important service to the urban community that some people feel a moral duty to support them.

FEEDING THE MIND IN THE CITY

Where cities grow, scholars cluster, and students gather to feed their minds. This has always been true, and is the reason for so many famous universities flourishing in the heart of cities; one of the great benefits of urban life is the easy access to learning.

WHETHER YOU ARE RETIRED and want to use your free time to pursue a new interest, hard-working but in need of another qualification, or simply restricted by family commitments or unemployment, there are great opportunities in a city, and many a small town to find the course of training or study that suits you. My own experience has been with lecturing to groups of adults for the Workers' Educational Association – always rewarding for me because the 'students', coming as they did from all walks of life with their own experiences, prejudices and interests, brought an enthusiasm to study and debate rather different to the one found among children. Whether my topic was an introductory course in astronomy or a series on Eastern religion, the

U3A

Recognizing the needs of retired people for opportunities of further education, a movement called The University of The Third Age was founded in France in 1973 and has since spread to cities around the world. Local education authorities also have a wide range of topics on offer for people who want to spend an evening a week with others, pursuing some mutual interest. This is education at its most fulfilling, feeding the mind and satisfying the spirit.

discussions were a pleasure, full of lively opinions – and unhampered by exams! Retirement can be a cause of great anxiety for people who fear an empty future. The pursuit of a new interest can transform their lives and become a mindful exercise in itself.

One of my oldest students, Lef, was ninety-two and the son of a rabbi. This was at the London Jewish Cultural Centre in Hampstead, where I lectured on 'The Evolution of Christian Thinking out of its Jewish Background'. Lef had memorized most of the Bible in Hebrew and would interject some beautiful quotations for us when they were relevant. I felt, as many do who work in the field of adult education, that it was a privilege as a teacher to have people like this in one's class, steeped in rich experience.

CHAPTER THREE

URBAN PROBLEMS

Urban living, it has to be admitted,
has problems. Those with children are keenly
aware of the risks that face a growing child in
the urban environment, while the fear of violence
and crime dogs the lives of many; we become nervous
about meeting the eyes of strangers, cautious about
getting too close to neighbours. For some people, the
very racial mix in a modern city, instead of being
something to celebrate, poses an imagined threat.
None of these issues need be a cause of anxiety,
however, and a mindful approach to living
will see them dissolve.

LONELINESS IN THE CITY

We have become, in the twenty-first century, a restless people who move home a lot, mostly for economic reasons, and that often leads to the breakdown of traditional family life, and to a sense of isolation and loneliness.

THE NOTION THAT 'MAN IS A SOCIAL ANIMAL' can be traced back over two thousand years to the Greek philosopher Aristotle; the actual word he used, 'politikos', carried the idea of being a citizen of the city. People are most fulfilled, and at their best, when they are members of a community with a network of human relationships, of friends, family and acquaintances. And yet, if we could produce a demographic map of the distribution across the world of lonely people, the numbers would cluster wherever there is a city; and not just because there are more people concentrated in one place. We are vulnerable creatures and a crowd of strangers is more likely to arouse feelings of suspicion and fear in us than of security and friendliness.

The city itself can generate and accentuate feelings of isolation. Physical proximity does not guarantee the sort of closeness we need to lead fulfilled human lives. Someone without friends in the country can blame their circumstances; someone without friends in a city is liable, tragically and often unreasonably, to blame themselves.

Lyrical Loneliness

It was in contemplating this sense of being isolated and alone, when part of the teeming multitudes, that led T.S. Eliot to conjure up that powerful image in *The Waste Land* of the early morning crowd flowing over London Bridge, moving as a mass to work. Watch a city crowd and often you will see blank faces, hurrying on, everyone avoiding eye contact. But the isolation of the individuals in the crowd does not end there: many take it home with them after the day's work is over.

It was the 1960s' pop group the Beatles, in their song *Eleanor Rigby*, who first awakened many of us to the pathos of someone else's loneliness. 'All the lonely people' is repeated throughout the song and it ends with Eleanor Rigby's death, relating poignantly that she was 'buried alone with her name'.

Vignettes of loneliness, images of young singletons, male or female, working at an unfulfilling job and returning to an empty flat at night to eat a solitary supper, appear often in poetry and are upsetting to contemplate. Equally saddening are stories of old people, living by themselves, perhaps after the death of a partner, and with no family or friends to care for them. They break the heart.

The Pit of Loneliness

The 'lonely hearts' columns in urban broadsheets reveal something of the size of the problem; full time work in a vibrant city does not bring with it protection from feeling alone in life. We touch here on the heart of one of the great human dilemmas: how do we relate to our neighbour? We live our lives alongside other people – in the family, in marriage, at work, out in the street – and in each case we are confronted by the incomprehensible mystery of someone else's conscious being. Each person is a world unto him- or herself, often hard to understand or fathom. How do we bridge that gap? How do we save another from falling into a pit of loneliness? And how do we protect ourselves from the same tragic fate?

Encounter with an Urban Saint

I was on an exchange visit to New York some time ago and teaching in a school on 92nd Street just off Lexington. In a lunch break, a senior Afro-American girl came and sat beside me – a friendly gesture from a pupil to a visiting teacher.

'Hi, Mr Ford! How are you doing?'

We exchanged pleasantries and then I asked her about herself and her plans. She hoped for Harvard and I could read from her demeanour and conversation that she had a good chance of a place. Then she told me that she was a Jehovah's Witness, which somehow I found surprising. I only knew of them as people who, uninvited, came knocking at the door to proselytize and sell their magazine, who didn't allow their children to celebrate Christmas, and who denied family members the right to blood transfusions when in life threatening situations – all negative associations in my mind.

Welcoming a New Neighbour

There are many ways to make a new neighbour to the street feel welcome. A colleague of mine adopted a lovely habit – she would appear on the doorstep of a newcomer after the removal van had gone and, while positively refusing to take up any of their time by crossing the threshold ('You are probably exhausted…'), would hand over a shepherd's pie ready to pop in the oven, with the words, 'Don't hesitate to phone or call if you need anything.' Not everyone followed it up, but a surprised gratitude was there and the gesture was, I'm sure, appreciated.

Other friends arrange a small drink party of local residents with the instruction: 'Please bring at least one useful phone number for [name], our new neighbour.' They also take photographs at the door and label them with their names as a gift for the newcomer.

So, what did it mean to her to belong to that faith group, I asked? I was getting ready to brace myself, hoping that my prejudices wouldn't show. I expected to hear beliefs I couldn't accept and an interpretation of the Bible that would irritate me.

'Well, Mr Ford – you have to know – this is a *great* city. I've grown up in it and I *love* it. But there's an awful lot of lonely people out there – particularly up in Harlem. So, at weekends, me and my mum go knocking on doors of some of those flats and invite them to join us at the kingdom hall. To find some friendship – you know?' She looked at me for understanding.

That was it. That's what it meant to her to be a Jehovah's Witness. I decided she was an urban saint. Who else would spend their weekends doing that? I have held a different view of Jehovah's Witnesses ever since (with a tinge of guilt about my earlier prejudices).

I had spent my life, until then, thinking that the various sects and faith groups that flourish in our cities were distinguishable by their teachings and belief systems. Much more important, I now realize, is what they have to offer their members in terms of human kindness, and how they view others out on the streets of the endless city.

BUILDING A NETWORK OF FRIENDS

It is important for our well-being that we are part of a community, for it is in relating to others that we begin to find ourselves. But living in a city can sometimes be difficult because there may not at first be any obvious community to which we can belong.

WE HAVE TO LOOK AFTER OURSELVES just as much as we need to care for others. The dictum 'Love thy neighbour as thyself' – one of the oldest laws in the Old Testament, highlighted by Jesus a thousand years later as a main pillar of his teaching – implies that we should also love ourselves. Self-love is not a selfish attitude; it is the basis upon which we can begin to love others. We should be able to smile to ourselves with warm pleasure that we are here, alive and living in the city. Life is good, and we are part of it.

One of the problems of urban life is that it does not always come with a sense of being a natural community. In this modern age, we move about so much that we often do not know our neighbours. Complete strangers live only feet away; we may hear their plumbing and their TVs but year in, year out, our paths don't cross. In the past, when people were born, lived, and died in the same place, a sense of community was natural; every individual had a niche and the unquestioned feeling that they belonged. Neighbours were known.

We should beware, however, of being too nostalgic about what could become a rather idealistic, rose-tinted vision of the past: life then had its own problems, which we need not enumerate here. The important thing is that we are alive *now* and need to be mindful of what that means; to be more aware, in our conscious living, of our circumstances and the opportunities that are open to us.

Choosing Friends

We arguably have the luxury, living in a city, of being able to choose our friends; many are of the opinion that this is far better than being part of a community like a village, where everyone knows everyone else's business. It can be inhibiting and hard to be yourself when eyes are watching from behind twitching curtains and everyone knows what you are up to. The anonymity of the city is a welcome relief to many.

We can build our own urban networks, create our own personal community of friends and contacts, but it takes time, creative energy and some tolerance. Widows and widowers, the newly divorced, young people moving into the city for employment – all these are potentially solitary people who need to be alert to the danger of sinking into a slump of victimhood. The victim thinks that circumstances have forced him (or her) into loneliness and feels sorry for himself.

The alternative to suffering alone is to make friends, with the emphasis on 'make' – they don't turn up on the doorstep ready-made. Making friends can be hard work for some of us, with many false starts and dead ends. We need to pick up on kind offers, follow the smile, be alert to other people, take time to talk to those we see regularly. There is no need to be pushy – just friendly and open, but sensitive to the neighbour who refuses to take the greeting or smile any further, respecting the desire that some people have for anonymity.

It can be good, too, to make the most of odd contacts – the quiet person at work who tentatively suggests meeting for coffee; friends with whom you have lost touch. It is worth remembering that many people one encounters are in the same boat and would welcome friendship.

Creating a Network

Madeleine Bunting, a regular contributor to the *Guardian* newspaper, has written of the gentle art of civility, so important
for the cohesion of neighbours (see the *Guardian,* 10 October
2011). It can be contagious. She tells of an elderly Turkish-
Cypriot neighbour who grew roses. Passing his house one
evening, she commented to him that the roses in his garden
smelled heavenly. He promptly went to fetch a pair of scissors
and cut the stem of a perfect red rose to give to her. 'It was
the start of a friendship between our families in which we
have exchanged recipes, herbs, spiced teas, cakes and flowers.'

Civility and small acts of kindness work well for the person
who lives alone. They lead to trust. The goal is to create a
network of dependable acquaintances whose company one
enjoys – friends to share gallery visits or to spend time with
over coffee; friends one can drop in on, or join on a shopping
expedition. It is a creative activity making friends, and one of
the best things we can do as human beings, an exciting project
that can enhance our lives. But we may often have to put ourselves out, and follow leads that threaten to be boring, accept
invitations we suspect of being dead-ends.

Many people who live alone discover that a good urban life
can be lived as a singleton. There can be great strength in
living by oneself. With a mixed network of friends they have
recreated the feeling of belonging – but on their own terms,
something our rural ancestors might have envied.

Coping with Empty Weekends

I used to dread weekends when, for a short period of my life, I lived alone: loneliness loomed with its attendant feelings of failure. The way to cope with it, I found, was to plan ahead, make a date with a friend for supper or a walk, cinema or gallery visit. One planned event like that could transform the whole weekend, giving me something to look forward to, and a peg to hold on to as my spirits began to rise.

THE FEAR OF STRANGERS

It is natural to be cautious of strangers when living in a city; we don't know what lurks behind the closed mask of a fellow passenger on the train, or the jostling pedestrian in the street. People pass by each other with glazed expressions, avoiding eye contact or any signs of friendliness.

EMOTIONALLY, THIS IS PROBABLY NECESSARY — it would be too exhausting to acknowledge the presence of everyone encountered during the day. But our anxieties can become excessive and an unreasonable obsession. We fear the rowdy gang at the other end of the street and take another route home. We hurry along at night by streetlight, fearful of dark doorways. Horror stories in the media, headlines of muggings and murders, are partly responsible, generating anxieties that are often completely unrealistic. Our lives may become dominated by suspicion and unease.

But a mindful approach to the urban environment will help remind us that the great majority of people are like us, going about their businesses, willing to be friendly, happy to be kind if the opportunity were to arise. We have, of course, to be sensible and alert to the obvious risks inherent in the urban scene, but without allowing those risks to play on our anxieties, or to inhibit the way we live.

The Good Samaritans

A very old friend of mine, in her nineties, left home one day with a letter to post; the box was only a hundred yards down the street. She was disturbed to see four young men with hoods loitering at the corner, and nervously crossed the road to avoid them. She posted her letter, and then, turning too quickly, tripped on the curb, fell, and banged her head badly.

She told me the story later, and of her astonishment when the four 'hoodies' came to her aid. They helped her up into a sitting position and sat beside her on the curb while they phoned for an ambulance. They stayed with her until the medics arrived and made sure she didn't leave her handbag on the pavement. It warmed her heart that lurking behind those threatening hoods there was nothing but kind neighbourliness. The fact is, there is more of it around than we think.

Parental Fears for Children's Safety

Given the media hype and front page headlines of knifings, shootings, gang violence and alcohol-fuelled sex, it is not surprising that urban parents worry about their children's safety and who they choose as friends. Urban life involves risks and there are no easy solutions on how to protect one's children. A mindful approach, however, will take *realistic* stock of the situation, being positive about the city (which is our home) while not allowing oneself to be driven to anxiety by the press's obsession with horror stories. A method I have found successful over years of being chaplain in a London day school for girls was to invite the parents of 13–14 year olds to an evening's discussion on '*The problems of bringing up a child in a city*'. I addressed them at the start of the evening, gave them a list of topics (on alcohol, dress code, travel arrangements at night, party going, friendships…) to discuss, and then divided them up into small groups of about ten parents (couples to separate to different groups!) and let them get on with it. I also invited some senior pupils to the evening and placed a couple of them in each group – this ensured that the discussion did not get out of hand! The pupils invariably became the stars of the evening!

FAITH COMMUNITIES

The good news is that we do not have to struggle on our own (unless we want to) when it comes to building up a community of friends in urban surroundings; many faith communities welcome new members with open arms and offer an immediate experience of belonging.

T HE CITY IS OUR HOME, NOT OUR ENEMY. The practice of mindfulness will help foster a sense of ownership. Our sense of identity comes partly from what has been called 'personal psycho-geography' – the place where we live giving us that inner reference point that contributes to feelings of belonging. We orientate our lives around home. For those of us who live in cities, that means the local patch of streets and pavements, back gardens and shops. This is where we belong and this is where we have to find ways to be glad.

That loose body of friends and acquaintances we build up through time (most of whom may have no link with each other), which becomes our own personal network, and from which we get a sense of belonging, is not the only way we may find to be part of the society that surrounds us. We can also have a sense of community by joining with others in a faith group of one sort or another. The Afro-American girl from Harlem reminded me of this, and made me rethink what I judged to be of most value in a faith group. Any religious tradition is complex and made up of many dimensions; there are its teachings and dogmas, its rituals and ethics, its social side and its sense of the transcendent. It is the latter two that have come to interest me most of all.

Putting Mindfulness to Work

The sense of the transcendent means different things in different traditions, but basically it is the belief that there is a 'beyond' in life; that there is more to being human than just the daily business of survival, more to the city than just the buildings and the crowds that temporarily inhabit them. Many would call this the spiritual dimension. For those who believe in God, it involves a personal encounter through prayer, perhaps with intimations of immortality; while for others, such as Buddhists, it is a spiritual reality understood in terms of transcendent peace. Whatever the tradition, practising mindfulness (which although coming from Buddhism is applicable to anyone's life, whether belonging to a faith group or not) is a way of becoming more aware of the surrounding city, understanding it and coming to terms with its reality, embracing it with love, establishing ownership.

Mindfulness in the city then calmly explores the streets with the mind's eye. It could involve visualizing a walk through familiar thoroughfares. For the Christian this may involve prayer, asking for God's blessing on networks of people, known and unknown, recollecting the suffering and loneliness, the anxieties and angers, the joys and sorrows of those neighbours with whom one shares the urban experience. For the Buddhist, it will be more a matter of extending feelings of compassion, to family, friends, acquaintances and, finally (just as importantly), to enemies. Bringing mindfulness to bear on the city, and to the fact that we belong to the city, is a way of dispelling ignorance (which clouds all our lives) while opening our minds and hearts to the reality of the life within and around us. It embraces the city with love (and as the Zen Master Thich Nhat Hanh might say, 'with a smile').

◆

'The practice of mindfulness defuses our negativity,
aggression, and turbulent emotions…'

FROM 'GLIMPSE AFTER GLIMPSE' BY SOGYAL RINPOCHE
HARPERCOLLINS, NEW YORK, 1995

◆

The Social Dimension

The second aspect of religious faith groups that I have come to value above others is the social dimension – the creation of a community, a family of caring people, to which one might belong. Whether it is in church, mosque, synagogue, temple or kingdom hall, these faith communities add immeasurably to the quality of urban life. They provide regular friendly contact with familiar faces of all ages, something that does not come naturally in the general bustle of the city; a weekly opportunity to exchange greetings, swap smiles and news, in a relaxed atmosphere with people we come to trust.

The best of these faith communities are those that look beyond themselves. They have become mindfully aware of the human needs of the city and respond with love, dedicating their time, energy and money. Groups like this can be found throughout the world, working with the unemployed in Chicago, with street children in Rio, or with the homeless in almost every city of the world.

Making the Connection

A classic example of such urban care, created by small communities within the city, is seen in the work of St Martin-in-the-Fields in my own London. This iconic Christopher Wren church stands prominently in Trafalgar Square, one of the best-known tourist spots in the metropolis. Less well known is The Connection at St Martin's, which does charitable work among the destitute and dropouts of the great city. It helps homeless people 'by providing specialist services – including a day and night centre, outreach for rough sleepers, skills training and career advice, activity programmes and specialist support for complex needs…'. The Friends of the Connection, an independent charity, are supported both by subscription and donation, and also by volunteers.

Those who are helped find warmth, security and support. Those who help have the satisfaction of knowing that they have 'made a difference' to the city they love – and discovered, perhaps to their surprise, a new community of friends.

Many charitable organizations are unrelated to any faith community, although some may have been so when originally founded. The work of the Samaritans, for example, the world's first crisis hotline, providing a friendly ear for those in despair, began in 1953 with the work of the Reverend Chad Varah from the crypt of his city church St Stephen Walbrook. Volunteers did not have to be trained counsellors, but simply caring human beings prepared to listen. The Samaritans has grown phenomenally since then and become a secular international organization handling hundreds of thousands of calls a year.

CRISIS AT CHRISTMAS

Crisis at Christmas began forty years ago in London. Volunteers give up any plans they might have for a private family celebration and opt to share their Christmas with the lonely and homeless, by helping to serve meals and provide warmth and companionship for those whose lives have been less fortunate. Both those in need and the volunteers have mushroomed in numbers over the years. In 2012 over 3,000 guests are expected at eight centres across London and 8,000 volunteers are required. The work of this national charity has spread to other cities such as Newcastle, Birmingham and Edinburgh, and has become dedicated to the greater vision of ending the scandal of homelessness in our society.

THE RICH RACIAL MIX OF THE MODERN CITY

◆

I firmly believe that one of the great contributions to urban life is the rich racial mix that characterizes most modern cities — the colourful kaleidoscope of faces, the snatches of unknown languages heard on the street, and the tantalizing smells that waft from ethnic restaurants: we are all people of one planet.

IT HAS BEEN CLAIMED that well over fifty different languages are spoken by the pupils of Holland Park Comprehensive School, Notting Hill, London — after English, the most common being Arabic (17 per cent) and Somali (4 per cent). Such is the urban mix in parts of London.

Take almost any modern city and examination will reveal the contributions made by different cultural groups; for example, the city of Bradford (a typical Yorkshire town) would not be Bradford without the contribution made by German Jewish migrants in the nineteenth century, or by the great influx of Irish after the potato famine of 1840. In the twentieth century, it was migrants from Pakistan who added to the diversity of the city; Bradford now has the third highest proportion of Muslims in the UK. This rich diversity is central to the character of the town.

The problem society has to face is not this exciting racial mixture but the minority of people who cannot cope with living next door to cultural variety. They continue to entertain the same fears those nomads experienced four thousand years ago when they encountered for the first time all the different languages spoken in Babylon.

A similar fear and ignorance of 'foreigners' drives some citizens into the hands of right-wing bullying groups (such as the British National Party or the English Defence League) who think they have a mission to purge society of everything they judge to be different. I have encountered these blinkered views all over the world, from Melbourne, Australia (horrified at the increase in the Asian community) to Buenos Aires (where Jews find it hard to gain acceptance for membership of some country clubs). The prejudices of people who do not question their own thinking can quickly be stirred up into racial hatred.

Breaking Down Prejudice

What can we do about these destructive emotions that poison urban living? How can different ethnic groups be accommodated side by side? The wall and the ghetto have been unhappy answers in the past. It is a fascinating reflection that the hub of the financial district in New York is Wall Street, named after the wall built by early Dutch settlers in lower Manhattan to protect them from the indigenous Native Americans, the Wappinger people. We think too of the crowded medieval ghettos where Jews were compelled to live, first in Venice and then throughout Europe, segregated from the rest of society for political and religious reasons, out of fear and a desire for control by other, more powerful groups. We think of the separate townships, for black and white, in South Africa under the apartheid regime. We may think too of the wall being built through Jerusalem today, segregating Arab from Israeli, which has to be seen, from any angle, as a tragic sign of failure.

Firstly, we may have prejudices of our own that need addressing. These can be dissolved through the practice of mindfully aware meditation – recollecting that we are one global community of human beings and that we share the city we live in. When shocked or upset by the views of others, we can of course always quietly question what we judge to be wrong thinking when we encounter it. A surprising number of people, when challenged, are ready to concede a point and think again – even if they do not admit it in discussion. Others, feeling strongly about racial hatred, are happy to join placard-carrying marches to denounce the excesses of xenophobic minorities. The danger of this method is that it can lead to an 'us and them' mentality, which does not always help.

Valiant attempts are now being made in the football world to outlaw racial chanting from the stands – and even racial abuse between players. This is bound to be an uphill task because racial feelings lie just beneath the surface in many a street culture; and they do resurface sometimes when emotions run high, both in the crowd and on the field. But with a TV audience of millions, football has to be a good place to start.

The Shared Approach

Personally I prefer a more 'behind the scenes' approach. Years ago, I was invited to take part in an initiative to bring together differing cultures in the large industrial towns of West Yorkshire such as Halifax and Huddersfield, densely populated places with all the problems of many larger cities. Evening meetings were arranged with invitations to Muslims, Jews and Christians. Each meeting was to discuss a topic where we shared concerns. A favourite subject was 'The challenges facing parents bringing up children in an urban environment' – it seems that all parents, whether Muslim, Christian or Jew, experience the same fears and worries, and are perplexed by similar discipline problems. They were wonderful evenings and some even got round to ending with prayer – itself a marvellous exercise in verbal tact.

Another approach, which I saw as a sort of 'oblique' education, gave me great personal satisfaction. I was chaplain at St Paul's Girls' School in West London – a school that we often regretted did not enjoy the racial mix and diversity of our near neighbour, Holland Park Comprehensive. So we performed an experiment – one that could be repeated beneficially, I believe, in any school.

I went to a wonderful map shop near Covent Garden and purchased the largest world map they had. I then went to a stationers and bought packets and packets of pins with different coloured heads.

Addressing the school, I invited everyone, teaching staff included, to collect four pins and stick them into the map to mark the birthplace of their four grandparents. Pins were colour coded for each year in the school (the staff room had its own colour).

This was to be fun – as well as educational – and no one was forced to take part, although the vast majority did so. Some children, for whatever reason, do not know where their grandparents are from and no one wanted to embarrass anyone over this. No one wants to draw attention to a mislaid grandpa or grandma!

The map was posted on a large notice board just outside my study. The first results were that I got some great feedback from parents who had enjoyed a family supper happily reminiscing over family history. Then over the following days I was able to eavesdrop on some delightful conversations: 'Where *is* Sheffield?'; 'Dad says Mum's mum was born in an Irish bog – where shall I stick my pin?'; and a Persian girl whispering to another with wonder, 'I didn't know there were so *many* of us in this school!'

Small crowds of kids stood around the map at lunchtime and during breaks, clearly astonished at what a mixed lot we were. With later class discussion, it seemed to be quite rare for a girl to have four English-born grandparents. If you go back in history only a short way, our ancestors were all immigrants, all 'foreigners'.

An Interfaith Peace Walk in Cape Town

Aslam, a relative of my son-in-law Shafeeq, once emailed me from Cape Town about an exciting interfaith initiative that could well be copied in cities around the world with similarly large racial mixes. The invitation to the 2011 event had a lovely human touch: 'You are warmly invited to join us on Reconciliation Day, 16 December 2011, for the annual Peace Walk from St George's Cathedral in Cape Town, starting at 09:00 and ending at around 11:00. Guest speakers are... *Bring water, a hat and comfortable shoes.*' This annual event had its roots in a mushrooming but effective interfaith movement against apartheid in the late 1970s. Aslam, himself a Muslim, writes: 'There were of course always expressions of religious intolerance from various quarters but these were always trumped by a very generous cross cultural spirit based on respect and mutuality.' The walkers walk together to three places of worship of the three Abrahamic faiths, Islam, Christianity and Judaism. 'We walk in silence and contemplation, and we succeed in establishing a type of walking holy communion for a couple of hours.' This, in my view, is community mindfulness at its best.

CHAPTER FOUR

RECREATION & WALKING IN THE CITY

*What first comes to mind when we think
of the city? For many, it is the continuous noise,
the roar of traffic and of aircraft coming in to land,
the urgent sounds of sirens; the merry-go-round of
lorries at building sites and the acrid chemical
pollution of the air — the relentless backdrop to
daily urban living. Yet there is another side to city
life. There are pockets of silence to be found and
opportunities to walk by riverbanks or beneath
the trees of a park, enjoying a fresh breeze.
The recreational possibilities are endless.
Wildlife abounds.*

BLURRING OF THE LINES

◆

Newcomers to urban life may at first despair that they have left the world of nature behind them; yet it only takes a little research to find places to walk in the city, in parks or by water, that are every bit as rich in wildlife as the countryside.

I GREW UP IN THE COUNTRY and sometimes found it hard to comprehend my father's nostalgia for the city scene. His childhood was spent in London and had he been a poet, he would have written lovingly about walking in the parks on autumn days when the low sun glowed red and the great leaves of plane trees drifted effortlessly to the ground; he even had fond memories of the fog, twisting about the lamp-posts and through the park railings at nightfall. Over the years, I have learned to love what he loved and to discover that the city is a great place for enjoyable walking. All of us, far too easily, make either/or judgements. The assumption about cities is that for a long walk you opt *either* for tramping along hard pavements, in polluted air, to the constant roar of traffic, *or* for leaving the city, perhaps for a weekend, to enjoy hedgerows bursting with flowers and birdsong.

In reality it is as easy to find wildlife, fresh air and some peaceful solitude in the city as it is in the countryside, but one has to seek them out. Urban dwellers can have both; they can enjoy recreation from their own doorstep.

Finding the Canal Towpath

One of the most peaceful places to walk in a city is along the
towpath of a canal, where horses, in the past, pulled the
barges. Many cities still have canals; we have only to think of
Amsterdam, St Petersburg or Venice – and Birmingham in the
UK is reputed surprisingly to have even more miles of canal
than Venice. The canals of London, which I know well, weave
almost unnoticed behind factories and storage depots, past
allotments and the ends of gardens. Flowers flourish along
their banks in summer – dog daisies, loosestrife and purple
mallow. Kingfishers flash by. Canals are used for recreation
now more than for industrial transport, but one meets so few
people that it becomes natural to say 'Hello' (something
urban dwellers often shun) when another walker passes. Even
just finding the way onto a canal can be fun. The entrance may
be no more than a small turnstile or unassuming set of steps
by a bridge. Silence descends as you leave the busy streets, the
traffic and the crowds, behind.

Discovering Wildlife in the City

It is part of Hindu mythology that the world repeats great
cycles of history, eras of golden creativity being followed by
eras of destruction and death, and that we are now at the end
of a great cycle and approaching the Age of Kali and the

disintegration of civilization. As we contemplate the daily news of urban riots, terrorism and the global spread of mega-slums, we might suspect that this Hindu mythology contains some element of truth. One of the sure signs of the onset of the Age of Kali, it was said, is that wild animals begin to roam free in the thoroughfares and back alleys of cities.

Are the foxes, hedgehogs and even badgers that slope through London parks and the bears that roam into the sub-urbs of some Canadian cities harbingers of doom? I can't help smiling at the thought.

The fact is, the world we live in is very different from any-thing imagined in ancient Indian mythology, when cities were small enclaves of order surrounded by jungles of untamed wilderness roaring with dangerous predators of every description. If the order of the city broke down in those times, the jungle would quickly have invaded, bringing 'nature, red in tooth and claw' to its streets. But the history of the world we live in today, marked by the growth of cities, is following a unique, and probably irreversible, trajectory, never before experienced in any era.

Wildlife is certainly invading our cities, but it is a gentler infiltration than imagined for the Age of Kali; and it is very welcome. The dividing line between city and country is becoming blurred, and when it comes to enjoying nature, it is far from being a case of either/or, town or field. The city has become the safe haven for many creatures that flourish well and are healthier – and live longer, in many cases – than their rural relatives. Hedgehogs wander through suburban gardens at night, while foxes breed beneath the garden shed. These days, the urban walker is as likely as his country cousin to be carrying a pair of binoculars.

City Birds

The blackbird, for example, a favourite English songster, is now a well-established city resident. It has an interesting story. Originally a woodland bird, this black thrush, with its powerful melodious song (good for establishing its territory among the treetops of European forests), began to move into cities in Germany early in the nineteenth century. It found a niche in the well-kept herbaceous borders and lawns of town gardens. Its song has become even more robust to overcome the noise of traffic and it is now one of the dominant voices in the urban dawn chorus. The bird is also a mimic: I have watched confused motorists at a petrol filling station trying to balance the air pressure in their tyres. While listening for the 'beep, beep, beep' from the machine, alerting them that they are up to pressure, an obliging blackbird on the wall behind gave a perfect rendition of the sound at random intervals. They have also learned to imitate the ring tone of mobile phones, temporarily causing more trouble – and entertainment. The blackbird 'singing at the break of day' has become as much an urban species as have we ourselves.

There are other success stories: black redstarts, normally making their nests on boulder-strewn hillsides on the Continent, quickly discovered that the rubble of wartime bomb sites provided an attractive breeding ground in London, and they have stayed. More dramatic still are the peregrine falcons (believed to be the fastest birds on earth) that have appeared in many cities, nesting high on the ledges of office buildings; while urban wetlands (some derelict, others carefully managed) offer safe havens for wild duck and occasionally more exotic species such as water rail or bittern.

Back to Nature

If mankind were to be wiped out by some Armageddon-like plague, nature would soon reclaim our cities completely. It used to be thought that rats would take over and become the dominant species. But rats are dependent on all the waste that a city generates and would quickly leave. Vegetation would spread rapidly from park and garden. The winners at first would be the grasses, together with banks of rosebay willowherb, brambles and purple flowering buddleia: absolute heaven for butterflies. In fact, butterflies are doing well in our cities already. Red admirals and holly blues, painted ladies and peacocks have all appeared in my city garden.

If mankind were to be wiped out... nature would soon reclaim our cities...

EXERCISE IN THE CITY

◆

The story of wildlife infiltrating and flourishing in London is echoed in other cities in England and throughout the world, so that walking in a city can be a rewarding experience and by no means a bar to enjoying the rich diversity of nature.

MANY PEOPLE WHO RETIRE TO THE COUNTRY find to their disappointment that their opportunities for walking are severely restricted by fast main roads and sometimes uncooperative farmers. They remember that there was a greater and more varied choice of walk back in the city. My own feet take me almost unbidden down to the river, where the light is magical and ever changing. In London, it is easy for me to plan a walk to fit into any time available – a short stroll to a riverside pub for a pint, or a longer walk to the next bridge and back along the opposite bank (offering the advantage of not having to retrace my steps). A really long walk might take in three or four bridges before crossing to return on the far side. The variety of river traffic – the small sailing boats and river steamers, individual skulls and practising eights – add life to the rising or falling tide; and the banks are rich with vegetation, purple valerian, weeping willows, and the scuttling of small animals. Pollarded poplars and plane trees line and overshadow the path in some parts. The further upstream one goes, the wilder the vegetation.

It's not just me – many people who have discovered the delights of a good city walk automatically make their way down to the river, wherever they are. I bump into them in places like Paris, by the Seine, captivated by the architecture, the artists' stalls and the constant call of the outdoor café.

In Western Australia, the Swan River, idling its way through Perth and down to Freemantle, offers a totally different experience. Here, walking in the evening and at weekends, I encounter families gathered to picnic and barbecue steaks after the heat of the day, beneath the shade of Moreton Bay fig trees, peppermints and river gums. Black swans sail majestically among the sailing boats and often a pod of dolphins will appear close to shore. Perth is a very open city, with a big sky and gloriously colourful sunsets, its fresh air blowing in from Freemantle as welcoming as its people.

The Walk to Work

I woke one day to the sound of happy chatter down in the street; the padding of little feet accompanied quiet giggles and the odd 'shush!'. Intrigued, I peered out of the window. A crocodile of young school children, with adults at head and tail, crossed the street at the road junction and disappeared round the corner in the general direction of Notting Hill.

A little enquiry revealed what was happening. A group of parents, fed up with London rush hour traffic and the dreaded drive to school, had decided to take things into their own hands and offered the walking crocodile as a solution to other interested parents. It was very popular. The children arrived at school well exercised, instead of tumbling sleepy-eyed out of a car; the dangers of a traffic jam outside the school gates were alleviated; car fume pollution was reduced – and money was saved. It was such a simple idea, requiring only the will and a little organization. The school was delighted.

There was one further benefit – the children would grow up with the experience of walking to work, and take it for granted as a natural activity. It can be as fast, if not faster, in the rush hour than using public transport and instead of being cramped together on a bus or tube with many others, some coughing or sneezing, you are out in the open, breathing your own air. Once you have mastered the route (and in the urban environment you will probably have many alternatives, some involving crossing the park or following the riverbank), you can time your journey to the minute and arrive exactly when you want to, unaffected by the vagaries of the traffic. The walk

'Why, Sir, you find no man, at all intellectual,
who is willing to leave London. No, Sir, when a man is
tired of London, he is tired of life; for there is in
London all that life can afford.'

SAMUEL JOHNSON (1709–84)
ENGLISH AUTHOR, IN A DISCUSSION WITH JAMES BOSWELL, 1777

Swimming

Walking, it is agreed by all, is a great way to keep fit; it costs nothing and exercises the body wonderfully well. However, I sometimes feel there is something missing and it is only when I go for a swim that I recollect what it is – my shoulders need opening out and my lungs extending. After a swim, my posture, both sitting and standing, is improved and I become more mindful of my breathing. In a city it is easy to find a swimming pool; many schools have taken to renting their pools out for swimming clubs, or for individuals in the lunch hour. Even more fun is to find one of those outdoor pools hidden away, often among trees, such as the bathing ponds up on Hampstead Heath in London. Personally, I find that half an hour a week (backstroke for me) is transforming and a great addition to my daily walk.

---

also offers you the chance to begin the day mindfully, quietly sorting through what has to be done, who has to be faced. And you will be fitter as a result.

Jogging in the City

There are many more opportunities to keep fit in the city than there are in the country; getting started and committing oneself to a routine is often the only obstacle to enjoying them.

Public swimming pools, sports clubs, tennis courts and cycle tracks – they all abound. Cycling is becoming increasingly popular as councils create safe cycle tracks throughout the city and its parks. Sometimes whole families can be seen keeping fit together, parents shepherding their children as they peddle erratically on their newly acquired bikes.

And then there is jogging, which, like walking, costs nothing. I am not a jogger myself, preferring a healthy walking pace; but I did once experience this form of exercise and found it strangely memorable. I was teaching in New York at the time and several colleagues were joggers, so I thought I'd give it a try. From a brownstone house on the Upper East Side I made my way down Lexington Avenue, up Fifth Avenue, and then across into Central Park. It was a great way to get to know the Big Apple and if I'd stayed I think I might have become an obsessive jogger. Images from those jogs still come to me thirty years later – the awe-inspiring buildings reaching high into the sky all about me; the faces I passed on the street; the feeling of being exercised and fit. It enhanced my feelings of being alive and living in New York.

One is sometimes forced to wonder whether jogging is really good for you – when middle-age anxiety drives people to put on running shoes, their bursting red faces as they pass by suggest they may be nearer a heart attack than health. But a keep-fit routine needs good sense; with wise guidance, jogging can be an excellent way to keep the body in trim.

Connecting with our Ancestors

We evolved on the savannah over two million years ago as endurance runners, able to outrun any animal. With naked skin and four million sweat glands, we can run through the heat of the day when predators and prey have their siesta. Large muscles in the bottom (the gluteus maximus) for balance, ligaments and muscles for holding the head steady, a long waist easy to twist as each leg pounds forward, strong hips and knees – all combine to make running as natural to us as breathing. No wonder little children run about so much – it is in their genes to do so!

Running in the early morning through the urban park for recreation, we are identifying with our distant ancestors in practising one of the most ancient of human activities – although without spear, or bow and arrow; and without fear of becoming someone else's breakfast.

Hopefully, the air we breathe will become cleaner and less polluted as technology advances. Highways and freeways are the lifeblood of the modern city and it makes sense, if you want to go jogging or cycling, to find a park as far away as possible from major highways or junctions. Pollution from autos travels further than we used to think and people with health issues should be aware of this risk.

And for those people who hate the idea of cycling or jogging, every city will offer multiple opportunities for good exercise routines with a teacher of yoga, t'ai chi or Pilates.

The Roar of the Crowd

A confession – I have never really been a team player, which I sometimes regret when I watch my favourites, Manchester United or Barcelona, move the football up the field with flowing elegance. Fortunately, not playing for a team does not disqualify us from enjoying team sports and it is in the urban environment that they flourish; cities support their teams with enormous tribal pride. Loyalties are passed down through families for generations. The occasion of a match, like all good drama, allows supporters to entertain and indulge powerful feelings of antagonism and competition, of 'Us' against 'Them'.

If you are an American lover of baseball, it may be the New York Yankees you support, the San Francisco Giants or the Boston Red Sox. Or you may prefer watching the gladiatorial spectacle of American football, the teams clad in safety helmets and massive shoulder pads; or following the athletic giants of basketball. There are too many team sports with home grounds based in cities to mention here; but the urban roar of the crowd is an experience that elevates the spirits of millions. The anticipation of going to an important match and the exhilaration of being part of a crowd do great things for urban morale. Even from a distance, I have found, there is something stirring and primal about the roar of thousands of supporters drifting up to my home in Hammersmith from Fulham Football Ground at Craven Cottage.

CHAPTER FIVE

VISTAS, CEMETERIES & OBSERVATORIES

Cities are a constant source of surprise —
you think you know your urban scene intimately
when suddenly a hidden gem is revealed, a secret
garden, charming café or ancient church. But who
would imagine how thrilling it is to snatch a fleeting
view of the landscape beyond the city; guess that such
rich pockets of flora and fauna survive in urban
cemeteries; dream that from the very heart of a modern
city we can gaze, in real time, into a gigantic cluster of
suns over fifty thousand light years away? We have to
let our urban focus relax to find these things.

THE CITY IN ITS ENVIRONMENT

◆

Living mindfully means learning how to stop our agitated daily activity to become more aware of ourselves as living, breathing human beings, creatures of the natural world, and members of the city. This will involve discovering how the city interacts with the rest of the world.

THIS THEN LEADS TO SOME QUESTIONS: How did this city grow where it is? What is its function and how does it relate to the countryside around it? No city exists in isolation from the rest of the world and it is good to begin to feel in our bones how dependent the city is upon the rest of the life of the planet. It is not a polluting oddity, stuck artificially into the landscape; the urban environment is itself a product of the natural world, strange as that may seem.

Every town, every city, grows somewhere significant – nestling in the protective hollow of the hills, or benefiting from being close to the sea, where ships can unload cargo; taking root at the junction of great rivers where trade routes cross, or near a coal mine or grain belt with all the employ-ment that industry and agriculture can offer. Many were originally placed strategically, providing protection for their citizens – walls of defence against enemies, bastions against armies. There is an obvious logic about the foundation and growth of every urban conurbation, and it takes only minimal observation, thought and reflection to tell us how the city lodges in the surrounding countryside, how it belongs in its own way to the planet.

It can be very satisfying and strangely pleasing to become aware of the way a city sits in its environment, whether it be the city where we live, our own familiar home, or a new urban landscape explored with open eyes for the first time. A rewarding aspect of mindful urban living is to develop an appreciation and understanding of the way the city relates to the land around.

Pausing to Absorb a View

A moment spent looking beyond the city can catch one unawares. Hemmed in by the jostle of strangers streaming both ways down the pavement; dodging deliveries staked by a shop door; peering into bookshops; walking past glass windows, our reflection moving with us – everything is close and busy, when suddenly, while crossing a street, carefully looking both ways, you catch an unexpected glimpse of a distant landscape, fields and trees far out of town.

These views have a valuable part to play in the way we live our urban lives. They may at first appear to be, but are not, moments of escapism. We can appreciate them, not because they remind us of the unpressured life we desire (though they may), the rural dream far from the gaol-fever of urban bustle, but because they inject new life into the urban scene.

A good place to contemplate the out-of-town scene in my local town of Lewes offers a seat on the pavement at a small table, and coffee. I often pause there for half an hour. The High Street is steep at this point. Mothers toil up the pavement with pushchairs; a traffic warden idles down the hill checking number plates, sometimes halting humanely to give a harassed shopper time to dash out from a shop with a purchase and drive away. Snatches of disconnected conversation catch the attention, the speakers lingering long enough to give one an entertaining hint of family goings-on; gales of laughter get lost among the roar of passing traffic. A tired shopper rests a clutch of bags by your legs.

But you hardly have to raise your eyes to look out and over the centre of town to see a high curve of downland, up above some houses and trees. An ancient burial mound, a tumulus dating back to the New Stone Age, is a small hump on the horizon; it carries your mind back in time for an arresting moment. I always rise from the coffee stop exhilarated – and it is not just the caffeine. My love of Lewes is enhanced by being able to gaze out to the countryside beyond; the town is improved by knowing how it sits in its landscape.

An Evening in Ayamonte

Almost all small towns share this ability to reveal the landscape around them – vignettes of far-off countryside caught in a glimpse and cherished. I have a brother who lives in Spain, in the Andalucian town of Ayamonte. Sit of an evening at a small table with a glass of wine in the sociable town square, where the loud chatter of sparrows in the manicured palm trees vies with the shrieks of happy children playing ball or roller-skating around and around in front of their families, and you might catch yourself gazing out of town.

A narrow side street, leading away from the square, runs west down to the broad Guadiana river and sailing boats. On the far bank of this slow tidal river is Portugal and the Algarve; a medieval castle rises above the salt marsh, built originally to guard the land against Spanish marauders. The castle becomes a silhouette as the sun sinks in that direction. You might see a skein of pink flamingos flying elegantly upriver, their long necks, extended legs and strange bills making them look cartoonish – like aerial hockey sticks with wings.

Views from the Larger City

It is not just small towns that offer views and vistas from the bustle of the street – many a large city does the same. Anyone who has ridden a streetcar in San Francisco knows the exhilaration of catching a view of the bay – of Alcatraz with all its mysterious history as a prison island, where the 'bird man' was incarcerated; or of the iconic Golden Gate Bridge. And in the afternoons the ocean asserts its near presence by the curling wave of sea mist that rolls in over the western suburbs. San Francisco would not be San Francisco without its hair-raisingly plunging streets and glorious views, or its prox-imity to the Pacific. It draws life from its surroundings, builds its character on things seen in the distance.

Sydney in New South Wales offers similar sea views beyond the ends of its thoroughfares. You step off the pavement to the encouraging 'get-a-move-on' sound of the crossing signal (I always think of the urgent laugh of a kookaburra), traffic halted and waiting, when mid-street you suddenly see, beyond the enormous overhanging limbs of a Moreton Bay fig tree, the harbour – blue water, sailing boats, a swiftly moving ferry; and beyond that the north shore at Manly. For a moment you are tempted to stop and enjoy the scene – but the engines of the stationary traffic are running, growling to be off, and so you rush on, the moment glimpsed and caught in memory like a butterfly in a net.

Every city has something to offer, whether it be the Rocky Mountains seen from Vancouver or the snow-covered Alps from Geneva. Every good view is easy to miss in a preoccu-pied life; even easier to ignore.

Views Over the City

People who have apartments in high-rise buildings can enjoy the opportunity of contemplating the way their city sits in its landscape every day. London lies in the hollow of the Thames Valley and there are many places from which the observer can get an overview of the city, get a feel of how it has been shaped and how it settles naturally into the local geography. From central London, such fortunate people have views of the suburbs rising up to the North Downs, or, in the opposite direction, the heavily treed slopes of Highgate and Hampstead Heath.

This view of London can be reversed. Instead of catching a glimpse of something lying *beyond* the enclosing buildings, revealed for a moment at the open end of a street, we may find ourselves looking out *over* the city, contemplating from above how it fits in its place in its entirety. Walk out of the woods on Hampstead Heath over the open grassland and all the major buildings of the metropolis lie beneath you – *there* is St Paul's Cathedral, there the Stock Exchange; there the inside-out shape of the Lloyd's building, and the new skyscraper affectionately known as 'The Gherkin'; 'The Shard' rises above them all on the South Bank, while the London Eye turns slowly like a great bicycle wheel, revealing similar views to tourists in its rising, then falling, pods.

Views of the city from above, or distant views from below but above the snarling traffic and the milling crowds, help the city to breathe and us to breathe with it. They are worth seeking out and cherishing.

Every city has something to offer, whether it be the Rocky Mountains seen from Vancouver or the snow-covered Alps from Geneva.

SURPRISED BY CEMETERIES

A cemetery is definitely not the first thing that comes to mind when thinking about a modern city with all its bustle, noise and movement. In fact, it is the opposite of all that marks the busy city; it is a place of stillness, peace and silence. There are paths for slowly strolling down and benches for resting.

A FEW YEARS AGO, an excited birdwatcher made a discovery in Stoke Newington, one of the most densely populated parts of London: firecrests were wintering in Abney Park, the local cemetery. Not many people have seen the firecrest, a tiny olive-green bundle of feathers smaller than a mouse, with a black line through its eye, a bold white eyebrow and a fiery red crest. It is Britain's smallest bird, an honour it shares with its cousin, the more common goldcrest. A few firecrests cross the channel from the Continent every year, but they usually fly south for the winter. A London cemetery, it seems, offered a comfortable alternative with its holly trees, firs and ivy-covered trunks. Since that first discovery, there have been many sightings of the firecrest in this and other urban cemeteries.

Paradoxically, urban cemeteries often teem with life, particularly if they have not been too 'well tended'. In London, jays and woodpeckers, warblers and titmice have made the trees their home, along with squirrels, flocks of roosting starlings, owls and many other species of bird; and in the undergrowth there can be badgers, foxes, wildflowers, ferns and several varieties of butterfly.

If one's interest lies in the colourful beauties of the micro world, then old gravestones provide a wonderful opportunity for studying lichens, those primitive plant forms (actually two different plants living symbiotically) that have done so much for the living planet by consuming rock and turning it into soil. The fact is, one can find more interesting wildlife in an urban cemetery than in many parts of the countryside.

Walking the Pages of History

Of course, there are other (and many people would think better) reasons for visiting a cemetery; they link us with past eras and remind us that a city is not static, like a marble monument – it is a process, always changing, growing, developing and replacing its parts like a living organism. A hundred and fifty years ago London was London, yet none of its inhabitants were the same people as live there today. A stroll among the gravestones and tombs of a cemetery can make you pause and stand and think – to be astonished at how many children of Victorian families died in infancy, or to be struck by the name of someone well known in history.

Visit Highgate cemetery in north London and there is the tomb (a place of pilgrimage for many) of Karl Marx, who unleashed an idea on the world that changed the lives, for good or ill, of billions. Or perhaps you would prefer to linger by the grave of a famous scientist such as Michael Faraday, or the novelists George Eliot (*Middlemarch*) or Douglas Adams (*A Hitchhiker's Guide to the Galaxy*). In Highgate you walk the pages of history.

Every cemetery has its own character, from those where wild nature is allowed to rule and trees grow crookedly from broken crumbling tombs, to others that are governed by a different ethic. Explore Arlington military cemetery, situated directly across the Potomac River from the Lincoln Memorial in Washington, DC, and you discover a well-manicured place where tidiness rules. Regimented rows of identical white tombstones mark the resting places of soldiers and service personnel from wars dating back to the American Civil War. The Iraq and Afghanistan wars are remembered here, and there are tombs to unknown warriors; there are memorials to the crew of Space Shuttle Columbia and to the 270 people killed in the bombing of Pan Am Flight 103. John F. Kennedy and his wife Jacqueline are buried here, while one area is dedicated to the graves of freed slaves. A nation's history is laid out with neat and controlled respect.

In stark contrast to Arlington military cemetery, with its wide open glades and its close cut lawns, is an extra-ordinary baroque and opulent necropolis in the heart of the Argentinian city of Buenos Aires – the Recoleta Cemetery. The Recoleta is a walled miniature city; to stroll around the narrow streets of this great mausoleum is a surreal experience. Elaborate tombs the size of small houses are protected by wrought-iron grilles; coffins lie on shelves behind glass doors. An air of melancholy hangs over the whole ornate complex, and cats sleep in the sun on the steps, while small rufous ovenbirds strut the pavements with their unexpected goose-step walk. Many of the best Argentinian families have used this cemetery; even the remains of Eva Perón may (or may not, for it is disputed) rest here. There are life-size marble angels at every corner, or peering down from above. A day's architectural delight awaits the astonished visitor. A quartet of Columbian musicians sang at the entrance gate the day I visited: I sat in the sun and enjoyed their performance.

THE JEWISH CEMETERY IN PRAGUE

The old Jewish cemetery in Prague is one of my favourites – small, and packed with character and history. It dates back to the fifteenth century (some would say earlier) and is dominated by ancient tombstones, crammed tightly together, owing to the Jewish custom of never removing a gravestone. Many of the stones sport small heaps of pebbles, revealing that the ancient practice of carrying, and leaving, a pebble when visiting a grave is still honoured. There may be as many as twelve layers of graves in this limited space.

LOOKING UP AT THE SKY

The city, we find, is not an enclosed space, an urban trap; it has windows looking out onto a wider world, onto surrounding landscapes; out into the universe itself. With only a little knowledge, the sky — seen from your doorstep or your garden — can become your own living, real-time, planetarium.

THERE'S A LINE IN *The Threepenny Opera*, by Bertolt Brecht and Kurt Weill, about the moon looking like 'a worn down old penny'. This image of the moon is recognizable to anyone who may catch an unexpected sight of it, distant, detached and silent, sailing high between the buildings of London. When the moon is round and full, it is smudged with dark patches. For some people, the patches delineate the face of the 'man in the moon', while for someone else, gazing up from the street of a Chinese city, they represent a jade hare (he who in mythology grinds in a mortar the seeds of immortality). We now know, of course, that these smudges are the ancient lava plains left to solidify after a great bombardment of asteroids 3.6 billion years ago, when the solar system was still young. They have been there, appearing much as they do to us as we pause and look up for a moment from the pavement, since before life began to evolve on Earth. The jade hare, the man in the moon — they have seen it all. They remind us human beings how new we are.

Following the Moon

We should not forget the sky when we think about the city sitting in its landscape. Leaning out from a hotel bedroom window in Venice, you may see snow on the Alps; from a street in Denver you can catch a glimpse of the Rocky Mountains – great distances by human standards. But from any town square, down any street, from even the smallest back yard anywhere in the world, you can gaze up at the sky. Once we know which way to look, we can keep an eye out for the new moon, monthly. It gives a rush of pleasure to see that thin thumbnail sliver of silvery white in the bright glow of an evening sky, taking the eye out and beyond the dark silhouette of buildings and high-rise blocks.

Look for it again; watch the moon change from night to night. In a few days the crescent is broader, revealing the first of the smudges (to the naked eye, a small, dark oval spot) that give that other world the appearance of a worn down old penny when full; this is the Mare Crisium or 'Sea of Crises', a hot desert of solidified lava, broken rock and dust, 555 km (345 miles) across, surrounded by mountains that reach 4,572 metres (15,000 feet). We can contemplate this gigantic plain directly, from the street outside our own front door.

A fortnight after being new, the moon is full, sailing serenely; perhaps behind passing clouds, stage-lit orange and purple from below by the lights of the city. We can still make out the Mare Crisium and many other ancient lava seas.

A splash of white, from near the moon's south pole, emanates from a massive impact made more recently in the moon's long history (only half a billion years ago) – Tycho, the mountainous crater at the heart of this extensive system of bright rays, could easily accommodate the whole of London.

Without the moon, we might not be here at all. It has been argued that it was the regular rhythm of the tides rising and falling that made it possible for early life to leave the oceans and continue its evolution on land. That 'worn out old penny', sailing silently beyond the clouds far above, has had a hand in who we are. The idea of *interbeing,* that our lives are involved with the lives of everything else in a complex web of interconnectedness, goes further the deeper we probe.

Observing the Night Skies

The Internet will quickly provide information on local astronomy groups. With them, you could learn how to follow the moons of Jupiter as they orbit the great planet; observe sunspots and eclipses; discover with the naked eye the faint patch of light that is the nebula in Andromeda, a galaxy of two billion suns over two million light years away.

You might join a shooting star counting party, meeting away from bright lights in a city park. A good night is 12 August, when shooting stars seem to emanate from the constellation of Perseus; one can see dozens of these Perseids in an hour, particularly from cities in the northern hemisphere. The nights leading up to 14 December are also good for shooting stars, when the Earth in its orbit around the sun passes through the disintegrated remains of an old decayed comet.

Observing the night skies, like discovering views out of town, can lift one out of the city without travelling anywhere. These experiences enlighten the urban life, revealing something of our place not just on the planet, but in the universe.

Telescopes Open to the Public

Many cities boast an astronomical observatory that will regularly open its doors to the public, giving non-astronomers a chance to view the heavens. Sydney, New South Wales, has such an observatory built before light pollution made it difficult to use the telescope for much serious work. It is very close to the famous and iconic Sydney Bridge. I found my way to this observatory a number of years ago with one wish in mind – to see Omega Centauri, a star cluster only visible in the southern hemisphere. The astronomers obliged! Omega Centauri is no more than a smudge to the naked eye, but through the telescope it revealed its majesty – half a million stars held together by gravity in a dense globular cluster. It was as though a heap of sugar had been dropped on to the velvet blackness of the sky, every sparkling grain a massive sun shining down on us from 15,000 years ago. Unforgettable.

CHAPTER SIX

THE CHANGING CITY: PAST & FUTURE

*Every city is a living structure and not a
static place — always changing, growing, developing
and evolving; sometimes dying. We have to share
this continuous change and learn how to embrace it.
The city is a process more like a human being than a
building; it has its own trajectory through history,
much as we do, and it is in the comings and goings
of its people that we witness the most important
part of its life. With care and understanding,
the city will grow well.*

THE EVOLVING CITY

◆

A mindful approach to urban living, while focusing on the gift of life in the present moment, waking up to the reality of the city and being glad to be alive in the here and now, also makes us aware that change and evolution are an inevitable part of the city's nature.

As WE HAVE ALREADY NOTED, it is estimated that, by the year 2050, 75 per cent of humanity will be urban dwellers. Our ability to accept change in the evolving character of the city will be partly dependent on our recognition of the fact that our urban living is part of an emerging process, a small chapter in a greater story of human history. We cannot preserve things just as they are, turning towns and cities into heritage museums on a large scale.

While contemplating the changing life of the city, it can be helpful to know something of its past before reflecting on ways it might evolve in the future.

Snapshots from the Past

As we become more aware of the city we live in, we might find ourselves asking questions about its past. It is easy, through the local library or the Internet, to find some answers. Each of us will take a different selection of mental snapshots from our reading. They will help us to feel that 'this is my home – this is where I belong'.

In my case, my mind turns to the river, the Thames — described as a 'forest of masts' in the sixteenth century, when the press of boats of all sizes, barges, lighters, tilt boats and ferries became so great that it was described as a 'jam'.

When walking the riverbanks upstream from Hammersmith, I often fancy a spot of 'mud-larking', seeing what I can find in the exposed mud at low tide. Stems of Victorian pipes turn up, and shards of pottery; but there is always the hope of finding something really ancient. Iron Age swords and daggers have emerged from the mud; polished stone axes from the Neolithic era have also been retrieved from the riverbed. Perhaps they were thrown into the Thames by people who loved it as I do, wanting to make an offering to the god of the river.

Another image that flutters through my mind is of pigeons with their wings burning, singed and smoking from the Great Fire of London in 1666. It was Samuel Pepys who observed and recorded this detail: he had taken to the river to watch the fire spread. Astonishingly, no more than ten people are known to have died in this historic event. Pepys himself lamented the losses of the booksellers. And that reminds me of an understated but remarkable event that happens every year – The Mercer's Company, an ancient city guild, makes a donation of books to the libraries of the two St Paul's Schools, to replace the ones lost in the Great Fire, when the boys' school was situated in the shadow of St Paul's Cathedral. What a spine-tingling link with history!

THE FEAR OF URBAN RIOTS

◆

Looking to the future, it is easy to be a prophet of doom, foreseeing increasing levels of violence on the streets of our bursting cities. Images of angry crowds hurling abuse at helmeted riot police are part of our daily news. We close the door, privately hoping the mayhem won't come our way, or spill down our street.

WE RARELY REFLECT IN TIMES OF PEACE on the importance of law and order in the modern city. It is a gift for which we can be grateful, but often just take for granted. The eruption of riots, whether provoked by some smouldering and underlying tension or simply the unintended consequence of the disintegration of a reasonable peaceful protest, is a reminder of the value of a robust social order. It seems sickeningly easy for that order to break down, and society to become vulnerable to the uncontrolled emotions of the few.

Rioting in London in the summer of 2011 caught everyone by surprise. Anger at the police over what was judged to be an unjust shooting escalated rapidly into rampaging crowds of young people smashing shop windows, looting, setting light to buildings; horrified audiences were glued to TV news screens dominated by the scenes of destruction.

Pundits in the media attempted to understand and debated the causes: 'An unheard generation.' 'They feel overlooked; no one cares. The world these youths live in is not the same as our world.' 'They have no control over their own lives, no employment, and so they want to make a mark, *their* mark.' 'Illiteracy and the feeling of powerlessness drives them.' 'The most dangerous thing on the street is not the knife or the gun – it's the mind of the marginalized young person.' And so on. Some outraged citizens showed less understanding (and a lot of blind anger), blaming the parents, while speaking about 'feral rats' and the need for harsh punishments.

The Silver Lining

Quite clearly there is a massive issue to be understood and addressed here; but it should be with optimism. More significant to my mind than the wanton flash of destruction was the response in neighbourhoods that had been trashed. In Liverpool, where the riots had spread, a group of young people, linked through social networking, came together after the mayhem, with brushes and brooms; 'It's my city,' said one, 'so I'm helping with the clearing up.'

Other groups, equally determined not to be victims, formed with the same purpose of sweeping up in other neighbourhoods, while citizens in Hackney reclaimed their streets by holding street tea parties to meet and discuss what had happened. They revealed a deep desire to understand – and to *act*. Citizen power! *This* is the way forward.

'It's my city … so I'm helping with the clearing up.'

DREAMS OF FUTURE CITIES

◆

There has been unprecedented change and development in cities in the past hundred years, due both to growth in the population and the use of new building materials. The human imagination is goaded to find a vision of the way the city might evolve in the future.

I N THE TWENTIETH CENTURY, many of these utopian dreams were dominated by ideas drawn more from science fiction than from any understanding of true human needs. Aerial taxis following automated flight paths filled the skies above a high-rise urban environment dominated by concrete, glass and steel; machines ruled the scene; people, as in many an architect's meticulous model, were added for effect.

Some architect's dreams, focusing more realistically on the human need for open space, trees and water, became a reality. The wave of British post-war new towns such as Milton Keynes struggled with a vision of the future, as did the new capital cities of Australia and Brazil – Canberra positioned strategically between Sydney and Melbourne, Brasilia in a carved-out space of the Amazon jungle.

One of my favourite utopian dreams comes from the nine-teenth-century pen of the artist, writer and socialist William Morris, who did not like everything modern, describing in his book *News From Nowhere* an underground railway carriage as 'that vapour bath of hurried and discontented humanity'.

He goes on to describe, in the same book, his socialist vision for a new society inhabiting a new London where money had been abolished and everyone worked willingly for the common good! The wonderful naivety of his vision makes me smile – and yet it is urging us forward to something that is right. Morris foresees a purified River Thames, where children can swim daily without fear of stomach upsets from polluted water and in which salmon swim upstream to spawn. Kensington and Notting Hill have become a great forest, in his dream; a natural playground for young people to spend their summers camping and enjoying good health. We need such bold blue-sky thinking to invigorate our dreams, if we are to take our changing cities seriously.

Citizen Power

Inspired by visions that may admittedly verge on the unrealistic, we can yet feel encouraged to take control, at least, of some local aspect of city life. Citizen power can be a great force for good when people work together with enthusiasm

'We will neglect our cities to our peril, for in neglecting them we neglect the nation.'

J.F. KENNEDY (1917–63)
US PRESIDENT IN A SPECIAL MESSAGE TO THE
CONGRESS OF THE UNITED STATES, 1962

and hope. And it is good for us all to feel some degree of ownership of our urban surroundings, as was expressed so dramatically by those armies of young people with their brooms, who turned out immediately to clear up the streets after the 2011 riots in London and across the country.

To take control, rather than to be a victim of circumstances, can be wonderfully empowering. Often it is the focus on one task that can be effective, as groups of volunteers have found in cities around the world.

The story of my old favourite, the River Thames, is impressive; described as 'a fermenting sewer' in the nineteenth century, when tens of thousands of citizens died of cholera from drinking its filthy water, and as recently as fifty years ago as 'biologically dead', the Thames is now claimed to be the world's cleanest river that flows through a major city. Dozens of species of fish have returned to its waters.

This impressive cleansing of the river has happened because people had the *will* to make it happen and for the government to legislate about the disposal of waste. The same is true of the 1956 Clean Air Act in the UK that outlawed the burning of fossil fuels within the city limits, thereby relegating the notorious choking pea-soup fogs to history. And often it takes just one person with vision to change the quality of urban living radically. The nineteenth-century epidemiologist John Snow was one such person; he recognized the link between the drinking of polluted water and the spread of cholera.

'As our homes become, above all,

places of investment, so do our cities.'

FROM 'GROUND CONTROL' BY ANNA MINTON
PENGUIN, LONDON, 2009

His discovery, at the water pump on Broad Street (now Broadwick Street) just by Oxford Circus in 1854, must have saved millions of urban lives in the past hundred years. The site of the pump should be a place of city pilgrimage.

Citizen pressure and the willingness of volunteers to turn out and lend a hand have transformed the quality of urban life in cities around the world – and will continue to do so.

ENEMIES OF THE CITY

In the past, walls, towers, bastions, and great gates locked at night protected many a city from its human enemies; but as we look back into history and then ahead to the future, we realize that the enemies of the city have changed.

THE MOST RECENT MANIFESTATION of these protective measures was the defence programme of the Cold War, whereby a shield of nuclear weapons was deployed in missile silo and submarine in a surreal balance of terror known ironically as MAD – Mutually Assured Destruction. Perhaps it is over-optimistic, as we increasingly think of the welfare of the planet in global terms, to believe that that period of history is coming to an end any time soon. But meanwhile the focus of defence has shifted somewhat.

Human error and selfish ignorance apart, the urban enemies today are of a different nature. There are, for instance, the seemingly increasing numbers of catastrophes inflicted by the natural world. 'Seemingly', because everything that happens is now widely reported live on TV; and also because, as the population of the world increases and migrates into the cities, the number of people affected also inevitably grows. The devastation of densely populated areas caused by earthquake, volcano or tsunami make for harrowing viewing, never mind the real consequences for the victims on the spot.

The people of Japan used to believe that earthquakes were caused by the wriggling of a giant carp imprisoned beneath the earth; we now know that the city of Tokyo is built on a tectonic fault line. Many other cities around the world that have grown near the sea are similarly vulnerable; Istanbul in Turkey almost certainly faces a major shudder in the not too distant future, as does San Francisco. A visit to Point Reyes in California, just up the coast from San Francisco, gives a salutary lesson in how nature can rip the landscape apart – in 1906 a massive shift in the Pacific plate caused a chunk of the State to jump north by 6 metres (20 feet), alarmingly displacing fences and tracks. The visitor can view them, now, in wonder.

Climate change will bring with it its own problems – rising sea levels in storm surges have already hit New Orleans and demolished the levees, and many other maritime cities are equally at risk. The last time global warming occurred was after the ending of the last Ice Age, when some early settlements were submerged; perhaps it was these that gave rise to the myth of the sunken city of Atlantis.

Internal Challenges

As we live our lives mindfully, we are bound to become alert also to the great internal challenges that face our growing cities. Quite apart from the discontents that lead to urban terrorism the world over, there are massive problems generated by the swelling populations of urban centres – the provision of workable infrastructures, power and transport systems; the provision of fresh water and food; and the disposal of waste.

At the more local level (which is where we all live), changes and improvements to the environment can be made if people make their wishes known and exert citizen power (through lobbying or joining groups of motivated volunteers). Many of our urban areas need regenerating; authorities who work together *with* property developers can ensure that whatever happens is a people-centred planning process and not one simply made with an eye to profit. We want centres that people like to visit, where they can stroll and shop in safety, with retail outlets that offer variety and character; and where they can sit perhaps in the shade of a tree. Many towns have already accomplished this successfully, with traffic calming measures and well-designed pedestrian precincts. Cities are always changing, and – just like their citizens – need regular health checks, which will only have any value when the citizens themselves are involved in the planning.

One development, which at first sight might appear to be beneficial but is causing increasing concern, is the building of gated communities. Public highways and public pavements are things we have grown up to take for granted, along with a public police force to patrol them. They offer a freedom of movement about town, which we have assumed to be a part of our urban inheritance. Shared space is what makes a city an exciting place to be. Gated domestic communities overlooked by CCTV, and gleaming new business districts owned by private corporations protected by their own private security companies, are a recent phenomenon; an idea imported to Europe from North America, where they were first developed. In a first flush of enthusiasm, they seem to offer something valuable. When I have stayed in Nairobi, Kenya, which has a high level of street crime, it has been a relief to be able to go out at night to dine in one of the secured districts, fenced in, with guards and gates. Many cities of the world have had to adopt this practice; it is sad that it has to be so, and a sign of a major humanitarian failure.

Similar developments in American or British cities are an entirely different matter. Homes built in gated communities offer those with the money to afford them a sense of safety, protection from the masses living beyond the gates. In reality, they increase levels of neurotic fear and encourage divisions within society; ghettos for the rich. They also limit and control the free movement of citizens.

What Lies Ahead

The way forward for urban living is full of uncertainty; but that is not in itself a bad thing. Creativity often happens on the fringes of chaos and there are lots of hopeful signs. Guerrilla gardening and beekeeping, volunteer clean-up groups, street parties and annual festivals are all indications that when people are motivated, they can change their environment for the better. I hear recently from a teenage cousin of 'yarn bombing', by which young people knit cosy covers for fire hydrants or leg warmers for the limbs of urban trees – slightly strange, perhaps, but heartening. And of authorities who've met the problem of graffiti head on by offering the walls of a whole street to graffiti artists. Inspiration and well wishing abounds, which brings optimism to our lives.

We need to foster this sort of positive thinking that embraces the future with hope – because it is almost certainly true that the fate of our fragile planet depends to a large degree on how we learn to live in cities.

BIBLIOGRAPHY & FURTHER READING

◆

London: The Biography by Peter Ackroyd (Chatto & Windus, London, 2000)

Thames: Sacred River by Peter Ackroyd (Chatto & Windus, London, 2007)

My Garden, The City and Me: Rooftop Adventures in the Wilds of London by Helen Babbs (Timber Press, London, 2011)

The Urban Beekeeper: A Year of Bees in the City by Steve Benbow (Square Peg, London, 2012)

The Endless City edited by Ricky Burdett and Deyan Sudjic (Phaidon Press, London, 2011)

Zen and the Art of Raising Chickens by Clea Danaan (Leaping Hare, Lewes, England, 2010)

Planet of Slums by Mike Davis (Verso, London, 2006)

Vegetable, Fruit and Herb Growing in Small Spaces by John Harrison (Right Way, London, 2010)

Emma Darwin: The Inspirational Wife of a Genius by Edna Healey (Headline Book Publishing, London, 2001)

Birds in London by W.H. Hudson (Longmans, Green & Co, London, 1898)

Urban Mindfulness by Jonathan Kaplan (New Harbinger Publications, Oakland, USA, 2010)

Going Solo: The Extraordinary Rise and Surprising Appeal of Living Alone by Eric Klinenberg (Penguin Press, London, 2012)

Ground Control: Fear and Happiness in the Twenty-First Century City by Anna Minton (Penguin, London, 2009)

News from Nowhere and Other Writings by William Morris (Commonweal, London, 1890)

The Miracle of Mindfulness by Thich Nhat Hanh (Rider, London, 1991)

The Art of Mindful Gardening by Ark Redwood (Leaping Hare, Lewes, England, 2011)

Glimpse After Glimpse by Sogyal Rinpoche (HarperCollins, New York, 1995)

The Little Prince by Antoine de Saint-Exupéry (Wordsworth Editions, Hertfordshire, 1995)

The Georgics by Virgil (Penguin Classics, London, 1982)

Online Articles

'A civil society needs the kindness of strangers and acquaintances' by Madeleine Bunting, 10 October, 2011, www.guardian.co.uk

'People out of touch with nature, warns Sir David Attenborough' by the Press Association, 1 December, 2011, www.guardian.co.uk

ACKNOWLEDGEMENTS

Many friends have contributed ideas for this book, for which I am grateful, but I particularly want to acknowledge the debt I owe to Monica Perdoni, commissioning editor for Leaping Hare Press, whose conception and inspiration it was in the first place. Her suggestions and encouragement have been invaluable (and her 'nana bread' delicious!). My thanks go, too, to Jayne Ansell and Jenni Davis, senior editor and copy-editor, who have guided me most helpfully, reigning me in tactfully when necessary. Thanks are also due to Ginny Zeal and Peter Bridgewater for their superb design.

INDEX

allotments 43–5
ancestors, connection 108
anonymity 23
Aristotle 74
art galleries 23, 52–5, 57–8, 61
astronomy 122–5
Asunción 58
Attenborough, David 21
Avedon, Richard 66–7
Ayamonte 114–15

Babbs, Helen 35–6
Baudelaire, Charles 55
bees 37–40
Benbow, Steve 40
birds 32, 34, 101–2, 118, 129
botanical gardens 57, 58–60
Bradford 90
Brighton 36
Brooklyn 41
Buenos Aires 91, 120–1
Bunting, Madeleine 81

canals 22, 99
Cape Town 58, 95
cathedrals 65–7
cats 32, 34
cemeteries 118–21
Chapman, Johnny 48–9
chickens 41–2
children 60, 84, 93
cholera 134–5
citizen power 131, 133–5, 137
climate change 137
community 23, 76–80
    faith 85–9
    gardens 45–7
    gated 138
    welcoming neighbours 77
Covent Garden 61
Crisis at Christmas 89
Culpeper Community Garden 46
culture 10, 11, 20, 38, 51–71
cycling 107

Danaan, Clea 42
Darwin, Emma 52–3
Davis, Mike 19
Dickens, Charles 68–9

earthquakes 136
Edinburgh Festival 63
education 70–1
Eliot, T. S. 75

Farmers' Markets 69–70
food 16, 43–5, 68–70
'Food From the Sky' 46, 47
football 92, 109
friends' network 78–82
fringe theatre 64
future cities 132–5

gardens 25–49, 57, 58–60
guerrilla gardening 48–9

'Happening' 63–4
Hemingway, Ernest 17
history 128–9, 134–6
Hockney, David 54

interbeing 20–1, 124
Ismaili Centre 33
Istanbul 32, 67, 136

Jbeil 13
Jehovah's Witnesses 76–8
jogging 106–8
Johnson, Samuel 105
Jones, Inigo 61

Kafka, Franz 56
Kew Gardens 59–60

Lewes 10, 114
Liverpool 131
London 9–10, 14, 15, 40, 90
    art galleries 53, 54
    canals 22, 99
    community gardens 46, 47

Covent Garden 61
Fire of London 129
food 68
  gardens 26–7, 28–9, 32–6
  Kew Gardens 59–60
  riots 130–1, 134
  river 103–4, 129, 133, 134
  St Martin-in-the-Fields 88
  views 116–17
  wildlife 118–19
loneliness 74–82

Manhattan 18, 40, 48, 66–7, 91
meditation 8–9, 30–1, 62
Mercer's Company 129
Mollison, Bill 47
Moon 122–4
Morris, William 132–3
mosques 67
museums 52–3, 56, 61

Nairobi 138
Natural Beekeeping Trust 39
New York 18, 23, 48, 56, 76–8, 91, 107
Nhat Hanh, Thich 20, 31, 87

oak trees 59
Omega Centauri 125

people watching 62–3
Pepys, Samuel 129
permaculture 47
Perth 104
piazza 61–2
Point Reyes 136
Prague 121
prejudice 91–4
pruning 31

racial mix 90–5
recreation 97–109
Redwood, Ark 31
religion 38, 65–7, 76–9, 85–9, 93
  Buddhism 8, 38, 86, 87
  interfaith initiative 95

Rinpoche, Sogyal 29, 30, 87
riots 130–1, 134
rivers 103–4, 129, 133, 134
rooftop gardens 28, 33, 35–7

St Martin-in-the-Fields 88
St Paul's Schools 93–4, 129
Saint-Exupéry, Antoine de 25
Samaritans 89
San Francisco 32, 115–16, 136
seed bombs 49
Seedy Sunday 36
Seville cathedral 67
shooting stars 124–5
Singapore 58
Skara Brae 11–12
slums 19–20
Snow, John 134–5
sociability 23
strangers, fear 82–4
street theatre 63–4
swimming 106
Sydney 57, 58, 116, 125

telescopes 125
Tokyo 136
Tower of Babel 16
transcendent 86

University of the Third Age 71
Urban Age Project 14
utopianism 17, 132–3

Varah, Reverend Chad 89
Virgil 37–8
Virginia creeper 28–9
vistas 111–25

walking 22, 54–5, 95, 97–109
Washington DC 55, 120
wildlife 21, 32, 97–109, 118–19
Winstanley, Gerrard 48
Wollemi pine 60

yarn bombing 139

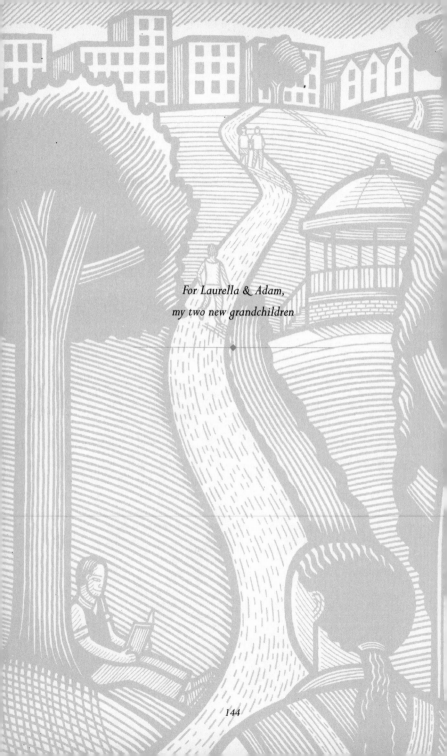

For Laurella & Adam,
my two new grandchildren